Policy-Making in Education

A Holistic Approach in Response to Global Changes

Miriam Ben-Peretz

ROWMAN & LITTLEFIELD EDUCATION
Lanham • New York • Toronto • Plymouth, UK

Published in the United States of America
by Rowman & Littlefield Education
A Division of Rowman & Littlefield Publishers, Inc.
A wholly owned subsidiary of The Rowman & Littlefield Publishing Group, Inc.
4501 Forbes Boulevard, Suite 200, Lanham, Maryland 20706
www.rowmaneducation.com

Estover Road
Plymouth PL6 7PY
United Kingdom

British Library Cataloguing in Publication Information Available

Library of Congress Cataloging-in-Publication Data

Ben-Peretz, Miriam.
  Policy-making in education : a holistic approach in response to global changes /
Miriam Ben-Peretz.
     p. cm.
  Includes bibliographical references and index.
  ISBN-13: 978-1-60709-160-8 (hardcover : alk. paper)
  ISBN-13: 978-1-60709-161-5 (pbk. : alk. paper)
  ISBN-13: 978-1-60709-162-2 (electronic : alk. paper)
  ISBN-10: 1-60709-160-7 (hardcover : alk. paper)
  [etc.]
  1. Education and state. 2. Education and globalization. 3. Educational change.
  I. Title.
LC71.B44 2009
379—dc22   2008053530

∞ ™ The paper used in this publication meets the minimum requirements of
American National Standard for Information Sciences—Permanence of
Paper for Printed Library Materials, ANSI/NISO Z39.48-1992.
Manufactured in the United States of America.

This book is dedicated to my husband, Moshe Ben-Peretz, whose constant support and encouragement accompanied my work all the way.

A map of the world that does not include Utopia is not worth even glancing at, for it leaves out the one country at which Humanity is always landing. And when Humanity lands there, it looks out, and, seeing a better country, sets sail. Progress is the realization of Utopia. (Oscar Wilde, *The Soul of Man under Socialism*, 1905, .40)

Contents

Foreword

Marilyn Cochran-Smith

The world we live in today is not the same as the world we inhabited ten, or even five, years ago. In today's globalized society, new markets, new media forms, and new trends in migration have created unprecedented challenges and new conditions of cultural, social, and environmental life. In particular, many new challenges have been created in education, and a whole series of complex new questions have become hot topics in the political and economic discourse: How should teachers be recruited, prepared, and retained in a global society? How should the success of teachers and schools be measured, compared, and rewarded? What (and whose) knowledge will be needed to solve problems that do not yet exist but will surely confront us as nations and peoples with differing agendas and interests? What is the role of educators and educational institutions in democratic societies, whether newly emerging or already existing? How do (and should) markets determine the ways schools and schooling are organized, funded, and accessed?

As many of these questions suggest, within the context of globalization, there is unprecedented emphasis on teachers, teaching, and teacher quality, and there are extremely high expectations for teacher performance in the twenty-first century. Based on the arguable assumption that education and the economy are inextricably linked, it is now assumed in many nations around the world that teachers can—and should—teach all students to world-class standards, serve as the linchpins in educational reforms of many kinds, and produce a well-qualified labor force to establish, preserve, or boost a nation's position in the global economy. This point was crystal clear in the 2005 Organisation for Economic Co-operation and Development (OECD) report, "Teachers Matter," which was widely disseminated and has been highly influential in discussions about education policy around the world:

> All countries are seeking to improve their schools and to respond better to higher social and economic expectations. As the most significant and costly resource in schools, teachers are central to school improvement efforts. Improving the efficiency and equity of schooling depends, in large measure on ensuring that competent people want to work as teachers, their teaching is of high quality and that all students have access to high quality teaching (OECD 2005, 1).

The last line of this quote from the OECD report touches on what I consider to be a central dilemma in educational policy and practice—how to ensure that all students have access to the kinds of rich learning opportunities that have historically been reserved for the privileged. This question is being taken up in different ways and with differing rationales and results in many nations, some of which have long had great diversity in the student population along with great disparity in opportunity and outcomes, and some of which have historically had highly homogeneous school populations but are now experiencing new waves of immigration and new patterns of cultural, linguistic, socioeconomic, geographic, and ethnic diversity across the school population. In this context, new concerns are emerging about the relationships of educational policy and practice, on one hand, and larger professional and societal responsibilities, on the other. Along these lines new questions are being asked about the social, economic, and institutional forces that constrain individuals' and groups' life chances.

Policy-Making in Education: A Holistic Approach in Response to Global Changes is a book that is made for these new times, a book located squarely in the middle of the many complex educational questions mentioned above. In this book, esteemed Israeli educator, Miriam Ben-Peretz, proposes a systemic, holistic framework for understanding issues related to educational policy-making in the context of the new demands and challenges of globalization. Drawing on decades of national and international experience, Ben-Peretz provides a readable and insightful description of the major facets of globalization at the same time that she problematizes this phenomenon and raises many questions about its impact on education.

In the first part of the book, Ben-Peretz takes up four key dimensions of globalization: demographic shifts brought about by changing patterns of migration worldwide; economic changes created by continuous global exchange and economic freedom, which are also the primary impetus for the counterglobalization movement; new information technologies that are rapidly changing our ideas about knowledge and knowledge production as new information channels are continuously produced and responded to; and environmental issues, in particular the degradation of the environment worldwide as a result of global warming, pollution, and the depletion of natural resources. Many others before her have described the forces of globalization. However, part of what is unique about this book is that Ben-Peretz argues that, and shows how, the dimensions of globalization are inescapably interdependent and interrelated to one another, and—even more importantly—she shows how these forces constitute the context in which today's and tomorrow's educational policy decisions are being made.

In the second part of the book, Ben-Peretz connects her analysis of the forces of globalization—for better or for worse—to the world of educational policy-making by focusing on three key aspects of schools and schooling: the curriculum, teachers and classroom teaching, and teacher education. As she does in her discussion of globalization, she shows how these three domains of education are ecologically interdependent and interrelated. The strength of the second part of the book is Ben-Peretz's skillful use of examples and cases to make her points. Although a wide range of examples are used, many of these are Ben-Peretz's own empirical studies and conceptual analyses, conducted over many years, of curriculum, curricular innovation and implementation, the practice of teaching, school organizational and social structures, schools as workplaces, and the roles of teachers and teacher educators in all of this—especially teachers' experiences, memories, and perceptions within and about those workplaces.

In the third part of the book, Miriam Ben-Peretz does what scholars seldom do. She links her theoretical framework for understanding education policy in a globalized world to concrete cases of policy-making on major issues. With two of the three examples she uses to make her case—an initiative to study and reform matriculation exams in Israel and a committee charged with restructuring the national teacher education system in Israel—Ben-Peretz herself played a major leadership role in the initiatives. With decades of experience as a university-based scholar and teacher educator as the backdrop, Ben-Peretz's insider status in the actual making of policy allowed her to write the third part of this book with unusual insight about the details of the policy-making process and provide a firsthand look at how the larger forces of globalization actually influence the concrete realities of practice and policy-making.

Ben-Peretz concludes her book with a comprehensive framework for understanding educational policy-making within the rapidly changing context of globalization. This framework is comprehensive in the sense that it pulls together the previous three sections of the book, each of which comprises an impressive amount of conceptual and empirical material in the first place, and joins these with the on-the-ground experience of working on major policy initiatives. The result is a set of deceivingly simple principles for policy-making in education that crystallizes key ideas: a systems or ecological understanding of education itself, a Schwabian or "commonplaces" perspective on the essence of policy-making, and a flexible view of policy implementation that emphasizes local, as opposed to presumably universal, educational contexts.

Policy-Making in Education: A Holistic Approach in Response to Global Changes is the latest in a long line of books, articles, chapters, and monographs by Miriam Ben-Peretz. Characteristically, Ben-Peretz takes up an extraordinarily ambitious project—linking the complexities of educational policy-making with the complexities of an increasingly globalized world. Also characteristically, Ben-Peretz pulls this off with intelligence (and wit) by combining critical analysis and synthesis of a wide array of scholarship with concrete policy-making experience. Overarching all of this is Miriam Ben-Peretz's stalwart commitment to enhancing students' (and teachers') learning opportunities and outcomes. This book should be widely read.

Acknowledgments

With deep feelings of gratitude, I wish to thank the people whose assistance was vital for this book.

Special thanks go to Tom Koerner, Vice President and Editorial Director of Rowman & Littlefield Education, who was ever ready to encourage, give advice, and respond to my many questions. I wish to express my sincere gratitude to Marilyn Cochran-Smith for her support and for writing the foreword to this book.

The contribution of Avivit Blanga to the research and writing of this book, as well as her enthusiasm for this work, have been invaluable, and I am deeply indebted to her. Special thanks are due to Madene Shachar for her dedicated assistance in the difficult tasks of typing, editing, and proofreading and her constant care for the bibliography. Many thanks to Meir Steinhart for his help in the bibliographic search. I thank Pieter Vanhuysse for his support and advice concerning my book. Heartfelt thanks to Dee B. Ankonina for her expert and insightful help in the editing of my book.

Finally, I wish to express my deep gratitude to my husband, Moshe Ben-Peretz, for his patient support throughout all the stages of this work.

Introduction

Globalization—a focal point of hostile passions and sometimes violent pro-
tests—has become a phenomenon doomed to unending controversy. Advocates cite its virtues and its inevitability. Opponents proclaim its supposed
vices and vincibility (Jagdish N. Bhagwati, writing in *Foreign Affairs*, 2002, cited
in Chanda 2007, 245).

The documentary film *Immigration*, created and narrated by Nitzan Horowitz (Israeli Television, channel 10, June 30, 2008), focuses on recent immigration from Africa to Spain. The film shows desperate people trying to
cross the Mediterranean in very shaky and crowded vessels with almost no
food or water. Many die on this route; others are saved by the Spanish bor-
der police and put in internment facilities. Yet many manage to leave Spain
and find their way into neighboring countries, like France, to work there
without official status in menial jobs such as cleaning, thus experiencing
the hardships of immigrant life.

This documentary provides insights into several phenomena linked to
globalization. For one, it exemplifies how environmental changes, such
as desertification in Africa, force native people to search for opportunities
in other countries, creating huge waves of immigration. At the same time,
this film shows how economic globalization, with its social and economic
gaps among countries and within countries, often leads to modern forms
of human bondage.

Globalization is highlighted by the emergence of three types of players: those
who globalize, those who are globalized and those who are left out by globalization. Those who globalize concentrate on capital, resources, knowledge
and the control of information. Those who are globalized are "information

poor" workers and consumers. Those who are left out have little or no access to information and knowledge, with no absorptive capacity as consumers and no relevance to production (Hallak 2000, 25).

Policies of education cannot prevent these situations but may play a crucial role in helping the various "players" respond more actively and effectively by creating awareness about these situations and by highlighting the desires of communities and individuals.

According to Geyer and Bright (2005), the integration of economy and communication all over the world has far-reaching consequences for humanity. Barnum and Walniansky (1989) relate to the inevitability of this process:

> Whether we like it or not, whether we understand it or not, it's happening all around us, 24 hours a day. Ideas, takeover plans and business are traveling east, west, north and south by telephone, fax and overnight mail, while goods, services and capital are circling the globe by airplane, ship and electronic transfer. These billions of crisscrossing transactions make up the process we call globalization, the vastly accelerated rate of business interaction that characterizes life on this planet as we head into the 21st century (Chanda 2007, 255).

The significant changes related to globalization that have fundamental ramifications for education may be conceptualized as four separate dimensions. The first is demographic movements, particularly massive immigration waves and the growth of multiethnic and multicultural societies. A second change concerns the transition into a globalized economy, with its accompanying impact on educational needs. Third, as new communication technologies become widespread, the modes of acquiring knowledge undergo rapid transformation, opening new horizons, on the one hand, but threatening, as well, the sustained survival of indigenous and minority cultures. And finally, not less crucial is the growing awareness of the dangers of environmental changes that seem to threaten the very existence of human life on planet Earth.

Leaders in education and policy-making must unquestionably address the extensive educational concerns emanating from these global changes; yet, I contend that such efforts must be conducted holistically, in order to overcome the fragmentation existing in the field of education. This fragmentation expresses itself in the predominant lack of coordination between the different dimensions of global change that face our society and the lack of integration between policy-making processes for the three major educational domains: curriculum, the role of teachers, and teacher education. The present book deals with all these themes and their systemic integration.

This introductory chapter sets the scene for the current volume. What is meant by the term *globalization*? How has globalization become such a contested phenomenon? Finally, what are the implications of globalization for policy in education? The chapter starts with some definitions of the term *globalization* and briefly mentions this process's historical roots. Next, several problematic dimensions of the globalization phenomenon are presented, along with their possible impacts on societies in general and on education in particular. This chapter also outlines the rationale for my proposed systemic, holistic policy-making approach as the central guiding framework for integrating educational domains to respond effectively to globalization needs. Finally, the introduction concludes by describing the different parts of the book and by highlighting their interconnections.

THE TERM *GLOBALIZATION*

The term *globalization* has received manifold interpretations and definitions. Some are general, such as "the act, process, or policy of making something worldwide in scope or application" (*Webster's New College Dictionary* 1995, 475), and others touch upon the range of components affected by globalization, such as "a phenomenon involving the integration of economies, cultures, governmental policies, and political movements around the world" (*Encyclopedia Britannica* Online 2008). Yet, globalization can also be defined through each single one of its features, such as the economical, technological, environmental, or social dimensions. For example, from an economical aspect, globalization is the development of an increasingly integrated worldwide economy marked especially by free trade, free flow of capital, the role of human migration, and the tapping of cheaper foreign labor markets (Mazlish and Iriye 2005, 8–9).

Over time, globalization has come to be seen as more than simply a way of doing business or a growth in immigrant movements. It has come to be seen as a process. Indeed, the word has taken on a life of its own, as shown by the *Encyclopedia Britannica*'s definition: the "process by which the experience of everyday life, marked by the diffusion of commodities and ideas, is becoming standardized around the world" (*Encyclopedia Britannica* Online 2008). Globalization, now understood as a vast, growing interconnectedness and interdependence, is an ongoing historical process.

HISTORICAL ROOTS OF GLOBALIZATION

[Globalization] is a process that has been going on almost throughout recorded history and that has conferred huge benefits. Globalization involves change, so it is often feared, even by those who end up gaining from it. And some do lose in the short run when things change. But globalization is like breathing: It is not a process one can or should try to stop; of course, if there are obvious ways of breathing easier and better one should certainly do so (Anne O. Krueger, First Deputy Managing Director, International Monetary Fund; cited in Chanda 2007, 271).

An account of globalization cannot be valid without considering its historical roots and its impact on present-day history. World history offers many examples of globalization in different periods and places. The book *Bound Together* (Chanda 2007) presents details about the ongoing process of globalization since the "African Beginning" in the late Ice Age:

> The period of divergence came to a close with the end of the Ice Age. Traders, preachers, soldiers, and adventurers from the emerging urban civilizations of the Levant, India, and China began connecting with one another, launching the process of globalization (XIV).

Chanda traces the growth of trade from the dawn of civilization to the present and the role of religious preachers in connecting different human communities. Adventurers such as Marco Polo and Ferdinand Magellan helped to integrate the world imperial rulers across the ages, from the Roman to the British Empire, promoting worldwide unity and exchange of goods. This process of increasing social and industrial trade, of course, accelerated in the twentieth century.

Not all globalization trends are expected or considered positive. Geyer and Bright (2005) present a view of world history in a global age as a course of events that disrupts expectations. Diffusion of industrial production, according to Geyer and Bright, has not served the integration of world economics into Western economies, nor has it subordinated non-Western warfare to Western command: "The mobilization of production and destruction thus turns out to be a globally unsettling process of unprecedented dimensions" (25).

Migration, a central component of globalization, has also changed dramatically in unexpected ways. Massive migration of Europeans to the Americas, and in lesser numbers to Africa, Asia, and Oceania, has been replaced by immigration to Europe and other industrial countries. Large-scale migration has become one of the essential dimensions of present-day globalization, along with several other dimensions.

DIMENSIONS OF GLOBALIZATION

According to Hallak (2000), the globalization phenomenon contains at least two main dimensions:

1. *The economic dimension.* Characterized by economic freedom, the global economy is spreading worldwide, both geographically and qualitatively. Today, technology, the norms and means of production, labor, and finance are being exchanged freely across borders.
2. *The technological and scientific dimension.* Portraying the expeditious development of technological and scientific innovations, this dimension mainly encompasses the field of communication, which sustains the power of globalization. Communication eases exchanges, speeds up production, and allows sharing of ideas, services, and goods. The global communication network offers its users multiple information options. At any time of the day, it takes only a fraction of a second to pass a message around the world or to access information.

In the first part of this book, I describe these two dimensions of globalization in detail (economics in chapter 2 and technology in chapter 3). Two other main dimensions—demographic changes and environmental degradation are discussed in chapters 1 and 4, respectively. The reason for including these dimensions is their utmost significance for today's policy-making in education.

The key characteristic of all these dimensions of globalization is their interdependence. For example, economic flow has led to a growing interdependence of companies and the creation of a global society that must continuously produce new forms of social organization and must assure the production of new knowledge and expertise. New forms of production and labor are closely related to immigration and have an impact on the environment. The various factors comprising globalization are interdependent and interact with each other in a state of synergy and synchronicity.

It is the weighty consequences of these interdependent globalization dimensions that render tremendous influence on the organization of today's society. Globalization clearly affects the most fundamental areas of human lives, thereby creating a need for individuals and systems to adjust and change so as to cope with the unexpected, novel, and dynamic situations triggered by global processes.

Nonetheless, "While globalization is clearly happening, its form and shape are being determined by patterns of resistance, some with more progressive intentions than others" (Burbules and Torres 2000, 18). Moreover, the rise of some new social movements and some trends in local and international nongovernmental organizations exerts an influence that may be termed "counterglobalization" (Burbules and Torres 2000, 18). The growing power of various "green" organizations is an example of such an influence. Thus, organizations and systems must take a stand where global processes are concerned, deciding whether to merely adjust to changes or to resist changes or to proactively predict changes and plan effective responses.

Hence, the inevitability of globalization has important implications for educational planning and policy.

GLOBALIZATION AND EDUCATION

The relevance of globalization to education and its impact on educational discourses has been increasingly recognized, as governments and business groups speak more and more of the necessity for schools to meet the needs of the global economy and the world (Spring 2008). The approach presented in this book calls for the recognition of the powerful impact that globalization processes are currently having on human lives worldwide and of the need to act promptly to envisage future trends and their effect on educational systems. In this book, I offer a framework for relevant policy-making in education against the backdrop of global processes.

Is it possible to predict the future of globalization and its evolving nature? Such predictions may be assumed to be a requirement for educational planning and policy-making. As educators, we should carefully examine how globalization affects education, or more precisely, "What are the changes likely to affect education systems in the coming decades resulting from globalization? And what kind of policy reforms should be adopted to address the consequences of globalization?" (Hallack 2000, 26). These are the themes underlying this book.

To address such policy reforms in education, the current book proposes a holistic approach that upholds the need for integration and coordination along several fronts. First, this central framework views the different dimensions of globalization as requiring connection and integration. Second, the proposed approach asserts that three major aspects of education that are vital for policy in education—curriculum, teaching, and teacher education—must also be integrated. Finally, the process of policy-making is perceived as requiring close interaction and coordination between diverse stakeholders and representatives of the different aspects of globalization. The structure of the present book corresponds with the need for integration along these three fronts, as seen next.

THE CURRENT BOOK

Educational literature concerning globalization tends to focus on the negative sides of this phenomenon. Still, policy-making in education cannot ignore global changes that are bound to have a far-reaching impact on individuals and societies in the twenty-first century. The current book provides an integrated view of the potential impact of global changes on today's policy-making in education.

First, discerning the need to delineate the relevant dimensions of globalization processes before proceeding to their implications on educational policy, in part I of this book, "Global Changes: For Better or Worse?," I briefly describe some global changes and their potential impact on education. The dimensions of global change that receive specific attention include changes in demographics (chapter 1, "Who Is Who in a Global World?"); the globalization of the world economy (chapter 2, "For Richer for Poorer, for Better for Worse"); the technology revolution (chapter 3, "The Information Highway: Where Does It Lead?"); and the issue of global environmental degradation (chapter 4).

Part I ends with some concluding comments, emphasizing an integrated, systemic approach to education. Such an approach views educational institutions and configurations in relation to one another and in relation to the larger society that sustains them and is, in turn, affected by them.

After the first part outlines the main dimensions of globalization as the backdrop, part II of the book, "The Magic Number '3': Coordinating Three Domains of Education in Response to Globalization," presents some literature on the three major domains of education that require integration and hold implications for policy-making: curriculum, teaching, and teacher education. Emphasizing the important interactions among the curriculum domain (chapter 5), the teachers' roles (chapter 6), and teacher education (chapter 7), this book draws a conceptual and operational map of the necessary coordination among these three domains. This map removes assessment and evaluation from their role as the starting point in policy-making. Instead, it views the image of the citizen of the future as the determining factor to be considered in policy-making.

Part II of the book presents some literature in education that has implications for achieving the goals of education agendas as outlined by the Delors Report (1996) for the coming decades: learning to be, learning to know, learning to do, and learning to live together. These goals cover essential aspects of education: identity formation, gaining knowledge, mastery of practical skills, and the highly important cultivation of interpersonal relationships.

Moreover, when referring to the links between globalization and education as in this second part of the book, it is pertinent to discuss which components of the education system might change following exposure to globalization processes. Hallak (2000) mentions five areas of concern for education policy makers:

- the goals of education
- the structure of the system
- the educators
- the assessment of programs
- the role of government and other protagonists

Part II considers four of these five areas. Goals, structures, and assessments are treated in the chapter on the curriculum arena (chapter 5). Educators are at the focus of the analysis of teaching (chapter 6) as well as in the discussion of the requirements of teacher education (chapter 7). The role of government and other protagonists is addressed in depth in part IV, within the proposed approach to educational policy-making.

Part III of the book, "The Anatomy of Policy-Making in Education: My Personal Experiences and Beyond," is a brief narrative of my own involvement in policy-making in education. This part of the book describes the role of the context and of individuals, as well as other forces, in shaping policy-making during a series of case illustrations._

Chairing policy committees is a complex and work-intensive position. The Ministers of Education in Israel tend to appoint committees whenever problems arise that require possible policy changes. The work and recommendations of such committees are expected to guide policy-making and to provide the basis and support for the decisions of policy makers. In the third part of the book, I describe and analyze two cases of chairing such policy-making committees—one on the reform of Israeli matriculation exams (chapter 8), and one on improving teacher education (chapter 9).

The committees presented in this section are examples of a naturalistic model (Walker 1971). A naturalistic model represents phenomena and relations that actually occur in educational processes, in this instance, policy-making processes. Walker's model is a temporal one: It postulates a beginning (the platform), a process (deliberation), and an end (design) of the product of deliberations, which might be a new curriculum or educational policy.

Part III also includes an overview of another major example of policy-making in education in Israel, which led to a structural reform of the education system (chapter 10, "School Structure Reform in Israeli Schools: An Example of Synergy in Education"). This example highlights some of the crucial issues in the planning and implementation of policies in education. The implications of these three committees' processes for policy-making in education in response to global changes are also noted.

In the final part of the book, "Policy-Making in Education in the Twenty-first Century," I present several models of policy-making, analyzing differences and commonalities (chapter 11). Factors and stakeholders that influence education policy are then discussed (chapter 12). Part IV concludes with a proposed holistic, systemic model for policy-making in education in response to global changes (chapter 13).

The epilogue at the end of the book mentions the double face of globalization as a catalyst for societal transformations, both positive and negative.

This last chapter calls for an appropriate response by systems of education, encompassing all three of its domains, to the possible impacts of globalization on the future of humanity.

It is my hope that readers of this book will gain meaningful insights into the complexities of globalization and the modes of policy-making in education necessary to effectively respond to these upcoming challenges.

I

GLOBAL CHANGES: FOR BETTER OR WORSE?

PART I INTRODUCTION

The first part of this book provides the background for the proposed model of policy-making in education. Four major global changes are identified and discussed in this part, and each chapter closes with these changes' potential impact on education.

I start in the first chapter with demographic movements that have altered the population landscape in many countries, having manifold implications for education. An estimation of immigrant population in 2005 suggested that about 190 million individuals were migrating at the time, constituting about 3 percent of the global population (U.S. Law Dictionary 2008).

The second chapter focuses on economic changes caused by globalization. These changes, accompanied by capitalist norms, constitute the main reason for contesting globalization and for the counterglobalization movements. Information technology is strongly related to the global market economy, and its ramifications are treated in chapter 3. The first part closes with chapter 4, on the threat of environmental degradation, providing examples of educational responses.

1

Demographic Changes:
Who Is Who in a Global World?

One of the major changes caused by globalization relates to demographic movements like migration. Migration may be defined as the movement of individuals and groups of people from their home countries or places of birth to other geographical locations. Another definition of migration is associated with worldwide movement from rural to urban sites. Such movements existed all through history, like at the beginning of the sixteenth century when millions of Europeans began migrating to the Western Hemisphere. Demographic mobility has significantly changed the map of the world, fostering multiculturalism.

From a historical point of view, three major varieties of migration can be differentiated (Gungwu 2005). The first variety is large-group migration of tribes, nations, or communities, which often leads to conflicts, conquests, or defeats (examples are the history of Rome, Britain, and Australia). Famines, plagues, or wars cause another variety of migration, as in the Irish famine of 1846–50 that brought more than 4 million Irish to the USA. Finally, Gungwu describes a third variety of immigrants, "sojourners":

> These were individuals and families who had not intended to migrate but left their countries to trade, to seek skilled employments, to escape temporally, or to look for adventure and fresh opportunities for betterment (Gungwu 2005, 105).

Nowadays, middle class and educated people tend to move from their homes to host countries that offer manifold opportunities for work and high standards of living. Gungwu calls this version "experimental migration" because many of these migrants tend to postpone their decision on whether to settle abroad permanently or return to their home countries.

Many of the migrants in the twentieth and twenty-first centuries experience discrimination in the countries to which they migrated. Cohen (2005) states:

> Whether it be Chinese in Malaya, Poles in Germany, Italians in Switzerland, Japanese in Peru, Irish in England, Palestinians in Kuwait, Caribbean peoples in Europe, Sikhs in Britain, Turks and Roma in Germany, or Kurds in Turkey—all these and many others experienced antagonism, legal or illegal discrimination, and have become the objects of violent hatred by majority populations (99).

Because of this situation, the diasporas—the scattered and dispersed groups of people away from their roots—tend to become an alternative form of social organization. Cohen (2005) argues: "Just as prior ethnic identities were not melted in the melting pot, so too did a diasporic consciousness survive in the interstices of the modern nation-state" (103). And yet, in spite, or maybe because, of the tendency of migrant populations to keep their ethnic cultural consciousness while living in another context, "Global diasporas have themselves become the sites for the creation and elaboration of new, original, hybridized cultures" (103). This may give reason for optimism: "Emphasizing the creative, enriching side of 'Babylon,' the radiance of difference, may provide a new form of universal humanism" (103).

> One might conceive of three common patterns of immigrant adaptation to a new society: 1) A pattern of acculturation and upward mobility, particularly for immigrants with skills and money, 2) A life of poverty and assimilation into the underclass, and 3) Delayed acculturation with economic advancement through consolidation with the immigrant communities (Barr and Lacey 1998, 2).

IMPLICATIONS FOR EDUCATION

Several questions are highly relevant to these migration processes, with ramifications for education. For instance:

> What are the hopes of various immigrant groups concerning an education? What kinds of values might schools give them that they might not otherwise have? What is the meaning of successfully achieving these goals within the immigrant community? (Barr and Lacey 1998, 4)

An important question concerns the relationship between education processes and the pattern of immigrants' adaptation to their new society.

Can education foster adjustment among immigrant children and even among their families? These questions are examples of issues that must be addressed by any policy-making process that aims to respond to the educational needs of immigrant students. However, a frequent problem that arises during policy deliberations concerns the extent to which policy issues are exclusive to immigration. It may be difficult to determine the extent to which policy issues relate to more general concerns in the majority population about education, poverty, race, and even the environment and the extent to which they touch upon immigrants' needs. Any education system that serves both local and global needs, attempting to meet the needs of specific populations as well as the needs of majority cultures, faces sizeable problems.

Immigration may result in the creation of multicultural classrooms that are characterized by diversity of ethnicity, religion, mother tongue, and cultural traditions. For instance, because of massive immigration from the former Soviet Union to Israel in the 1980s and 1990s, a typical classroom today might include up to 30 percent new immigrant students.

Imagine an elementary classroom with thirty students in Israel where the teacher has to deal simultaneously with four children from Ethiopia who speak Amharic, ten children from Russia who still have difficulties with reading and writing Hebrew, and a large group of Israeli-born students who are able to comprehend a difficult Hebrew Bible text. Comparable classroom situations might be found in other immigration countries, as well.

This diversity poses crucial problems and dilemmas for education. For instance, should immigrant students be immersed in mixed classrooms upon arriving in the new country, or would it be better to organize separate induction opportunities? Should schools make an effort to maintain the mother tongue of immigrant students? The following part of this chapter presents some studies related to these issues, highlighting the difficulties of planning and implementing appropriate educational policies.

IMMIGRATION AND EDUCATIONAL POLICY

Widespread immigration tends to lead to culturally diverse student populations in public schools. This situation adds a difficult burden to teachers' already heavy workload, even causing burnout (Tatar and Horenczyk 2003). The assumption of educators and policy makers is that immigrant students are disadvantaged and demonstrate lower academic achievements than their native peers (Zhou 2003). Teachers might be seen as lacking the knowledge and competencies that are required for teaching in multicultural classes (Shamai and Paul-Binyamin 2004). Yet this is not necessarily so. Eisikovits (2008), for example, reports that academic excellence coexists with cultural isolationism among transnationalist immigrant students who migrated in the aforementioned large-scale immigration wave from Russia to Israel. Eisikovits (285) quotes Remennick (2002, 525), who claims that:

> . . . young people who immigrated at high school age and above are almost as determined to remain "Russians" as are their parents. Although they master Hebrew rather quickly and generally do well in school and in college, their informal social networks remain mainly co-ethnic.

Such a situation may be common in other countries characterized by large-scale immigration. Eisikovits sees the following implications of her study for policy-making in a globalized world:

> As globalization expands, with multitudes of international experts, high-tech specialists, academics, and others on the move, culturally and ethnically retentive high-achieving immigrant students, like the RIS [Russian immigrant students] portrayed in this study, will become an increasingly conspicuous presence in schools of the future the world over. Educators will be confronted with this new form of cultural diversity. Multicultural teacher trainers should pay attention to this phenomenon and address it systematically in both pre-service and in-service contexts (288).

Nowadays, globalizing effects have produced many countries' experience of "transition," a process of change from one set of conditions to another, such as the transition of former socialist countries to capitalism. In these countries, globalization has far-reaching implications for the educational system, such as the spread of private education institutions. The biggest growth areas might be private schools at the nursery and higher education levels. In Russia, for instance, there are now 200 nonpublic tertiary institutions, more than the total number in Western Europe.

Other important outcomes of global changes, such as decentralization, relate to curriculum issues. China, for example, that used to be known for its uniformity of syllabi and textbooks, now has an open policy on textbooks and their content (Cheng 1997):

> Curriculum reform in some countries, most notably Armenia, Georgia, Moldova, the Ukraine and the Baltic States, has provided an opportunity to reassert a sense of ethnic or national identity using local, national or indigenous languages as the medium of instruction or as the main language to be taught. . . . In the area of curriculum reform, therefore, it can be seen that the transitional and transformational states are pursuing different routes, depending upon how far the authorities wish to redress past grievances and injustices. However, there is a recognition that, faced with the challenges of the global economy, there needs to be greater flexibility regarding what is taught and how students

are encouraged to think if they are to acquire jobs in rapidly changing labour markets (Watson 2000, 59).

On the other hand, the spread of English is part and parcel of the globalization process as it rapidly becomes the predominant global language. These contradictory trends—both decentralizing and centralizing—must be taken into consideration when planning policy in education in response to global changes.

WHAT CAN BE LEARNED FROM RESEARCH ON EDUCATION OF MIGRANTS? THREE STUDIES ON IMMIGRANT EDUCATION

The following are some examples of immigration studies and their relations to education policies and practices in countries with large-scale migration.

Study 1: Immigrants' Achievements in Mathematics

The first study compared mathematics achievements among immigrants to Israel from the former Soviet Union who were studying at school levels comparable to their homeland versus immigrants from Ethiopia who lacked comparable school experiences versus native Israelis who had studied in the Israeli school system. The study compared achievements in grades 5, 9, and 11. Several hundred students of different origins participated at each grade level. The instruments were developed specifically for the study because no other standardized instruments, or instruments that provided accommodations for immigrants from the former USSR and Ethiopia, were available.

In the development process of the instruments, immigrant teachers from the former USSR and Ethiopia were consulted on the presentation modes, language, and genres of the test items as well as on its contents, alerting the team to possible difficulties and/or suggesting accommodations. The national supervisors who were responsible for the national curriculum in math examined the tests, and their recommendations were incorporated.

Special attention was given to the tests' utilization of simplified and frequently used vocabulary that was assumed to be familiar to the immigrant students. In addition, Ethiopian or Russian names were used throughout the instruments in order to create a realistic and familiar sociocultural context. Further, in order to avoid working with a particular representation mode with which immigrant students may not be familiar, a variety of item modalities were used as test items, such as open ended, multiple choice with/without a need to explain the choice, and items that had one or more correct responses. The reliabilities of the math tests for the different grade levels were high, ranging from .94 to .97.

The results showed consistently distinct achievement patterns for the three groups, where scores of the Ethiopian students were consistently and significantly lower than those of the Israeli-born students, in all achievement measures (total score, problem solving, and mathematics communication and its subtests). Among students from the former Soviet Union, the achievement pattern of the ninth graders differed from that of the fifth graders and that of the eleventh graders. The ninth graders from the former USSR scored equally well as their Israeli-born peers in most measurements and even outperformed them in one subtest. In contrast, in the fifth and eleventh grades, students from the former Soviet Union scored significantly lower than their Israeli-born peers, namely, on all the specific measurements of problem solving.

The poorer scores among the youngest group could be explained by the link found between mathematics achievement levels and children's years of residence in Israel. These data indicated that immigrants required a substantial number of years, between five to seven, to reach achievement levels similar to those of native-born students. One explanation for the decline in achievements found for the eleventh graders might be the much higher content and skill requirements at that grade level.

Study 2: Immigrants' Perceptions of Classroom Situations

The second study concerns the difficulties that immigrant students experience in their new classroom environments. In the paper, "Tensions between Cultures in Educating Immigrants in Israel: From the Melting Pot Ideology to a Multiculturalism Orientation," Levin and Ben-Peretz (2007) examined the perceptions of classroom situations among immigrant students to Israel from the former Soviet Union and Ethiopia. This study had two objectives: (a) to examine immigrant youth's perceptions of their new classroom situations, encountered in a residential school in Israel; and (b) to compare these current perceptions to their perceptions of their prior classroom situations in their homeland (Ethiopia or the former Soviet Union). The assumption was that the findings would contribute to a deeper understanding of new immigrant students' absorption processes in school.

The most striking finding of this study was that the students from both the former Soviet Union and Ethiopia criticized and rejected the modes of teaching and classroom management in their new environment. Accustomed to a more rigid and strict classroom in their homelands, students perceived the nonauthoritarian approach of Israeli teachers in the youth village as "non-teaching," as "playing," and as lacking in explicitly defined subject-matter knowledge. The open classroom climate was interpreted as "laissez faire," implying that rules of classroom management might be broken. This perception manifested itself in the disobedient classroom behavior of immigrant students. As shown in the following excerpt translated from Russian by Steinhart (2000, 223), the students interpreted teachers' teaching style as an opportunity to challenge the school authorities:

> . . . yes, now I remember. There was disorder because of the singing and game playing in class. There was an argument among the students because there were those who wanted to learn in the usual way like in Russia and they went to talk with . . . the counselor. They told him that this way we are not learning anything and it is like a Kindergarten and not a school. Then he went to talk to the principal and with the teachers and there was a huge mess. . . Me? No, I love the fooling around and the games. . . .

These results can be attributed to educators' lack of knowledge regarding the appropriate accommodation processes for mainly low-Socioeconomic status immigrant students, who bring different learning styles, prior knowledge, cultural habits, and experiences to the classroom. Concerning immigrants' interpretation of classroom situations, it is worthwhile to open up discussion with students on the different meanings that students and teachers hold about concepts of teaching and learning, teacher and learner. Such discussions are likely to uncover hidden cultural dimensions and reveal different expectations, norms, and behaviors, thereby deepening levels of acquaintance, awareness, and respect between all students and the teachers, with regard to cultural diversity and to common needs.

In developing appropriate and effectively designed coursework for immigrant students, curriculum planners must consider students' emotional and sociocultural needs and furnish linguistic and academic support while stimulating students' cognitive development. Nevertheless, as seen in the connection between math achievements and length of residency in Israel in Study 1, even with the best curricular methods specifically targeting immigrant students, these youngsters do generally require a long time in order to adjust and perform equally well as native-born students in different school subjects in their new educational system.

Study 3: Immigrants' Adjustment

A third study concerns "Survival, Adjustment, and Acculturation of Newly Immigrated Families with School-Age Children: Cases of Four Korean Families" (Cho and Shin 2008). The number of Korean immigrants in English-speaking countries is growing. In 2005, more than 20,000 Korean students in grades K-12 left South Korea to study abroad. This qualitative study examined four Korean migrant families' experiences in the United States through observation, interviews, and orally told stories. The experiences of these families showed individual differences: Some children struggled, whereas others adapted more quickly into American culture.

Living in a new society involves redefining roles and adjusting to new roles and new lifestyles.

Cho and Shin's case analysis of these four Korean families raises some fundamental questions such as: What is education? or What is a good education? Does a good education refer to a good educational system, a good curriculum, and good attitudes among teachers in U.S. schools, or should it also include other attributes like students' feeling contentment in school, having friends, and adjusting to the culture?

Understanding these aspects of education may serve to address the needs triggered by the growing globalization of education through the initiation of better support systems and teaching styles. Moreover, it is crucial for educational planners to simultaneously adapt the curriculum content to meet the educational needs of citizens in the twenty-first century.

In concluding this chapter on widespread migration as a major global change and its impact on education, it is important to note a significant development in the perception of the human species. Because of the aspects of globalization that affect the entire population around the globe, humanity is confronting new circumstances:

> . . . Humanity, in short, does not form a single homogenous civilization. But in an age of globality, the humanity that inhabits this world is no longer a universalizing image or a normative construct of what some civilization or some intellectuals would want the people of this earth to be. Neither is this humanity any longer a mere species or a natural condition. For the first time, we as human beings collectively constitute ourselves and, hence are responsible for ourselves (Geyer and Bright 2005, 29).

These authors go on to state:

> This conclusion underscores both the promise and the challenge of the twentieth century as an age of world historical transition—that, in forging a world in which "humanity" has become a pragmatic reality with a common destiny, we do not arrive at the end of history. World history has just begun (29).

CONCLUDING COMMENTS

In facing the demographic movements that characterize today's globalization processes, paramount importance should be attributed to raising awareness among educators and policy makers regarding the difficulties confronting systems of education as they endeavor to effectively absorb immigrant students. Policy makers should attend to issues of multiculturalism, language acquisition, and modes for advancing achievement, as well as diverse school norms. This situation is exacerbated by the impact of new socioeconomic gaps created by economic globalization, which lies at the focus of the next chapter.

2

Economic Globalization: For Richer for Poorer, for Better for Worse

> There is nothing simple about the way that people in organizations, including schools, either learn about or try to respond to a changing world. Our capacities to understand, to learn and to respond are all limited in important ways. Yet the change is occurring, and schools are faced with the problem of what to do (Levin and Riffel 1997, 17).

One of the dominant global changes occurring concerns economy: "Globalization is above all an economic phenomenon that is spreading worldwide" (Hallak 2000, 22). Hallak distinguishes between two modes of economic globalization: One mode is spreading geographically, with millions of citizens all over the world working today in a globalized economy. The other mode is spreading qualitatively because, formerly, only goods, services, and capital crossed borders, whereas today all factors of production are exchanged, including technology and labor. As mentioned in the Introduction chapter of this book, according to Hallak, "the main characteristic of globalization is the interdependence of its different dimensions" (23).

> A kind of huge technological web is being woven over the planet, covering all aspects of human activity. For instance, at an economic level, new norms of organization of economic activity are generated every time new models of production based on knowledge and innovation are discovered (24).

These new norms of economic activity create an integrated global market economy across nation-states, as noted by Raduntz (2007):

> . . . Economic analysts see globalization as constituting the emergence of an integrated global market economy in which production and trade are rationalized

across nation-states and rendered "flexible" in order to respond to the rapidly changing economic circumstances aided by the new communications and information technology revolution (233).

In economic terms, globalization means a change in workplace organizations and a reorganization of the production process:

> . . . a reduction in barriers to the free flow of goods, workers, and investments across national borders; and, correspondingly, new pressures on the roles of worker and consumer in society (Burbules and Torres 2000, 14).

This phenomenon is related to potential issues concerning the dissemination of capitalist ideologies. "The term 'globalization' has come to express the phenomenon of the capitalist market economy's expansion worldwide and its penetration in to almost all aspects of social life" (Raduntz 2007, 233).

In political terms, the exponential growth in the capitalist market economy has led to a certain loss of nation-state sovereignty due to factors such as prolific trade exchanges, minimal governmental involvement, and the establishment of global economic and monetary regulatory institutions like the World Bank and the World Trade Organization (WTO). At the same time, globalization may be expressed by neoliberal reformist ideology in terms of individualism and competition consumerism, which may enhance individuals' initiative, creativity, and self-reliance.

Yet, the economic dimension of globalization, especially the crisis of the welfare state due to minimal government expenditures, has exacerbated a worldwide dichotomy between the "haves" and the "have-nots." Raduntz (2007) argues that the structural relations of the capitalist mode of production account for inequities between producers and consumers and between developed and underdeveloped countries. Large-scale economic growth has been accompanied by increases in worldwide poverty and environmental degradation, which activate significant global concern (Beck 2000; Raduntz 2007).

One reason for this concern is the growing gap between rich and poor and between societies and individuals who enjoy a better life because of globalization versus those that seem to be doomed to ever-worsening conditions. As a result, new social movements and nongovernmental organizations such as Amnesty International and environmental organizations such as Greenpeace have sprouted up all over the world. These organizations, among others, try to ameliorate some of these threatening situations.

McCarthy and Dimitriades (2000) see a link between the pressures of globalization and what they call "self-serving diversity." Self-serving diversity may express itself in the tendency of individuals to move ahead on the social ladder without considering other persons' situations. At a nation-state level, this self-serving diversity may be maintained through the acceptance of large socioeconomic and ethnic gaps.

ECONOMIC GLOBALIZATION AND EDUCATION

Global economy presents a serious challenge to education: to grant the citizens of the future, all citizens, an education that will help them success-fully steer a course within a rapidly changing socioeconomic world. The influence of economic globalization on education is far-reaching, through "... increased commodification of education, as well as calls for 'reform-ing' education in response to the supposed imperatives of 'globalization'" (Morrow and Torres 2000, 51). Education, then, tends to become a site of "unbridled consumerism—shopping for individual futures" (McCarthy and Dimitriades 2000, 188). For example, one of the outcomes of the marketization process, according to Raduntz (2007), is the marginalization of educators in favor of trainers and business managers and the rise of an instrumental model of education. This instrumental orientation manifests itself in an emphasis on school subjects identified with present-day eco-nomic requirements, like computer science, while diminishing the place of humanities in the curriculum. Another consequence of this instrumental tendency is the increasing role of standards and assessments in schooling.

The implications of the global informational economy model for oc-cupational structures and educational demands are significantly different from those proposed by "postindustrial society" models, as Castells (1996) argues on the basis of detailed comparative analysis: "The appropriate distinction is not between an industrial and a postindustrial economy, but between two forms of emphasis from *postindustrialism* to *informationalism*" (Castells, cited in Morrow and Torres 2000, 34, italics original). The grow-ing importance of information technology changes on the one hand (see chapter 3) and advances in modes of industry on the other places new demands on education systems.

One of the major problems while considering the relations between glo-balization and education involves:

> ... distinguishing more clearly between the fiscal crisis of the welfare state (which forces a reduction of expenditures irrespective of ideological leanings) and the presumed pressures of globalization that entail a reorganization of the production process and the subordination of education to it (Morrow and Torres 2000, 45).

Morrow and Torres (43) argue that:

> In this context, bilateral and multilateral organizations (most importantly in education the role of the World Bank and UNESCO) have a strong presence in the formulation of educational policy, more so under contexts of financial austerity and structural reforms of the economies.

The presence of powerful external donors "may lead to a process of public policy planning through marketing, rather than rational public choice and planning" (Morrow and Torres 2000, 44).

Still, it is of the essence to realize that:

> In an important sense, identification or understanding of issues and changes is always local. The literature on schools and change may talk in terms of macro trends—changing technology, changing patterns of work, changing modes of organizing. But what people actually see in their daily lives are local and concrete manifestations of larger trends. We may all agree that "the global economy" is an important change affecting education, but the meaning of this phrase will be quite different in a large urban centre and in a small rural community (Levin and Riffel 1997, 14).

The problem, then, arises of how policy-making in education can consider both global issues and local needs. The policy-making model outlined in part IV of this book attempts to meet this challenge by incorporating representatives of specific contexts, such as municipal leaders, into the process. The relationships between "economic globalization; the perceived redefinition of education; and the consequences of this redefinition for teachers' work" have far-reaching outcomes for education (Ben-Peretz 1999, 951).

In their book, *Re-Making Teaching: Ideology, Policy and Practice*, Smyth and Shacklock (1998) claim that "as western economies now position themselves in terms of improved international competitiveness, education and skill formation are major features of this process of structural readjustment" (18–19). They argue that this competitive process results in teachers' loss of their role as educators in the full sense of the word—as teachers involved in the moral aspects of teaching in order to create a more just and equitable society. Their book advocates the inclusion of teachers' voices in any consideration and deliberation about teaching and learning. The policy-making process elaborated in part IV of the present book applies this recommendation, upholding that the perceived role of teachers is one of the main challenges posed by economic globalization.

In order to foster equity as well as quality of life and environment, education systems must globalize moral concerns and cosmopolitanism, cultivating a sense of responsibility for humanity at large—a worldwide cultural community. This might be the most pressing goal of education policies.

CONCLUDING COMMENTS

The far-reaching impact of capitalist economic globalization on lives of people is cause for global concern because of the exacerbation of existing inequities. Moreover, economic globalization has transformed much of educational endeavors to serve market competitions. The moral voice of education has been muted, and teaching has become standardized. Modern technology plays a central role in this process, as seen in the next chapter.

3

The Information Highway: Where Does It Lead?

"You won't believe this, Mom, but today at school we learned about a new technology called 'paper and pencil!'"

Information technology is developing at a speed never before imagined, and, in a bizarre turn of events in the not too distant future, young children may actually come home from school bubbling excitedly to their parents about a "new" paper-and-pencil technology, as in the above scenario.

The modern world is undergoing a fundamental transformation as the industrial society that marked the 20th century rapidly gives way to the information society of the 21st century. This dynamic process promises a fundamental change in all aspects of our lives, including knowledge dissemination, social interaction, economic and business practices, political engagement, media, education, health, leisure and entertainment. We are indeed in the midst of a revolution, perhaps the greatest that humanity has ever experienced. To benefit the world community, the successful and continued growth of the new dynamic requires global discussion (World Summit on the Information Society 2003).

What could education contribute to the successful growth of this new dynamic? This chapter explores global technological changes and their potential impact on policy-making in education.

WHAT DOES "TECHNOLOGY" MEAN?

There is a lack of consensus on any one definition of technology, and, in fact, the Ministerial Technology and Design Working Group, established in Northern Ireland in 1991, asserts that imposing any particular narrow definition of technology is inappropriate (Gibson 2008). The Group suggests that technology could perhaps best be defined as:

> . . . based on applied science and [having] a demanding intellectual, creative, philosophical and human content. It is essentially pragmatic in nature [. . . and] includes those design activities which strive for technical excellence in terms of function, safety, reliability, quality, efficiency and economy (Northern Ireland Curriculum Council 1991, 6).

Such a broad definition includes, as well, information technology. Information technology has several goals: communication of information, sharing of knowledge, and narrowing of geographic and cultural gaps. The development of binary computer language has created a common "'linguistic currency' into which messages can be 'translated' for delivery through a variety of different delivery systems" (Boyd-Barrett 2000, 523). "The linking of computer technology with telecommunications has resulted in what is often called the 'information superhighway,' which offers a wide variety of information, communication channels and services" (Chronaki 2000, 559).

It is important to remember that "technology has to do with the tools and materials that are used for the creation of meaning" (Boyd-Barrett 2000, 523). The main goal for the use of information technology, like the main goal of education in the new age, must remain the promotion of "meaning making," allowing deep understanding of knowledge claims and modes of knowing. New modes of "meaning making" have the potential to promote economic development. Still, this should not detract from other directions of human development.

Information technology is not spread out evenly over the entire planet. There are "haves" and "have nots" in accessing and mastering this arena.

GLOBALIZED TECHNOLOGY AND DEVELOPING COUNTRIES

> The international transmission of know-how, knowledge and technological expertise is growing and it is increasingly important in the world economy (Archibugi and Pietrobelli 2003, 861).

The paper cited above argues that the globalization of technology offers new opportunities for economic development but that these ". . . are by no means available without deliberate effort to absorb innovation through endogenous learning" (862). The bulk of technological activities is produced and exchanged among developed countries, eliciting the question: How can developing countries bridge this gap? One way suggested by Archibugi and Pietrobelli is through global technological and scientific collaboration:

> Cross-border technological collaborations, in industry and in the academic community, appear to benefit both the parties involved since they allow an increase in learning and an exchange of information. Each country has an advantage to become a junction of techno-scientific information. In order to be engaged successfully in these collaborations, it is however relevant to have appropriate institutions . . . (Archibugi and Pietrobelli 2003, 878).

These prerequisite institutions, referring to academic research centers as well as to teaching organizations, are not easy to establish. Communication networks, with all their power and potential, pose substantial hurdles when planning collaboration. According to Castells (1999):

> A network is simply a set of interconnected nodes. It may have a hierarchy, but is has no centre. Relationships between nodes are asymmetrical, but they are all necessary for the functioning of the network—for the circulation of money, information, technology, images, goods, services, or people throughout the network. The most critical distinction in this organizational logic is not stability but inclusion or exclusion. Networks change relentlessly: they move along, form and re-form, in endless variation. Those who remain inside have the opportunity to share and, over time, to increase their chances. Those who drop out, or become switched off, will see their chances vanish (IV).

Thus, the essence of the new information network is not its stability but the status of being included or excluded. Social development in the twenty-first century depends on individuals and societies becoming and remaining a part of the evolving communication network:

> The reintegration of social development and economic growth in the information age will require massive technological upgrading of countries, firms and households around the world—a strategy of the highest interest for everyone, including business. It will take a dramatic investment in overhauling the educational system everywhere (Castells 1999, IV).

Overhauling educational systems is a highly problematic issue, as documented in the literature on reform and on policy-making in education, and as discussed below. (Parts III and IV of this book present evidence concerning the difficulties inherent in changing educational systems.) For one, the aforementioned lack of consensus regarding a single definition of the term *technology* complicates the process of introducing technology into education (Gibson

2008). Still, policies of education must address these issues if educational systems, and indeed whole societies based on the education of youth, hope to remain inside global communication networks. The present chapter does not attempt to solve these problems but rather aims to provide some insights into the present-day situation as far as educational efforts are concerned.

INFORMATION TECHNOLOGY AND EDUCATION

Information technology literacy means an ability to fluently use present-day technological innovations on the one hand and the knowledge about when and why such innovations could be used on the other. Literacy in this arena includes, as well, the development of critical abilities; for instance, to judge the reliability of information gleaned from online sources. As suggested by Leonard and Salzman (2007), technology education must be undertaken with caution to avoid a strictly financial perspective that aims solely to harness technological power in order to achieve worldwide financial dominance. According to these writers, in the global world, technological education should be considered as a mandatory prerequisite for success but should be the share not only of aspiring engineers but also of all students across the board.

Leonard and Salzman suggest the following aims for technological education: "Educational institutions should . . . focus on educating the types of technologists and innovators that the markets will demand through gaining better understanding of changing job requirements and employer needs, rather than relying on their longstanding curricula and programs" (13). In other words, technological education should include not only sufficient mastery of the technological tools themselves but should also train students in the necessary skills for analyzing and predicting marketplace innovations as well as for developing and managing globally networked teams.

Clearly, policies of education cannot ignore the technological revolution and must take steps to adapt to the new world in which we all live, but in doing so policy makers are faced with a myriad of challenging questions. How can technological education be accomplished effectively? Are computers in classrooms a sufficient response? Should technological education be introduced directly into the curriculum, and if so, how? What could be some basic principles for educating people to live satisfying, productive, and human lives while engulfed by a stream of unending digital messages sent by information communication technology?

A case in point within the field of technology education is the concept of "media education":

Media education seeks to increase children's critical understanding of the media—namely television, film, radio, photography, popular music, printed materials and computer software. How media texts work, how they provide meanings, how media institutions and industries are organized, and how audiences make sense of media products, technologies and institutions—these are the issues that media education addresses. It aims to develop systematically children's critical and creative powers through analysis and production of media artifacts. This also deepens their understanding of the pleasure and entertainment provided by the media. Media education aims to create more active and critical media users who will demand, and could contribute to, a greater range and diversity of media products (Bazalgette 1989, 1, cited in Boyd-Barrett 2000, 513).

For example, with regard to students' critical understanding of the Internet, Wallace and Kupperman (1997) found that:

Pupils' learning can be naïve and superficial when "surfing" the web pages. In a particular web-based ecology project, sixth graders were not found to be reflective or critical but instead they seemed mainly to take online information at face value without evaluating the source (Chronaki 2000, 564).

Critical thinking is essential for evaluating information and its sources and for making defensible choices. The above excerpts emphasize the value of instilling critical thinking in students so that they can relate more productively to media in its manifold forms.

However, the critical thinking aspect of media education alone does not sufficiently address the crucial issues at hand in terms of the dynamic changes characterizing human communication of information and the world's growing reliance on a computerized knowledge base such as the Internet. These changes require new media competencies in order to be able to participate in the new digital environment, with its potential for human development as well as its many inherent risks. Such an approach to technology education also introduces social and cultural issues. For example, Internet users may forge connections with people all over the globe, but at the same time these users become exposed to the risks of forming dangerous relationships. In addition, an overreliance on the ready information supplied by the Internet might lead to a decrease in individual creative work. Therefore, policy-making in education must account for the personal, social, and economic costs of ever-increasing hours spent on the computer, such as neglecting intimate human companionship, contracting health problems due to a more sedentary lifestyle, and relinquishing connections and responsibilities to one's local community.

CURRICULA AND THE TEACHER'S AND
LEARNER'S ROLES IN TECHNOLOGY EDUCATION

Interesting policy questions pertain to the curriculum. Should technology education be taught across the curriculum or as a separate subject? Is it a solely practical field, or does it encompass theoretical components, such as sociology or psychology? Psychological frameworks, for instance, could include the study of perception or the limits of knowledge. Should practice illustrate or exemplify theory, or should students become practitioners of technological competencies without necessarily addressing theoretical frameworks?

A chapter by de Vries (2000) on technology education elaborates on such issues and problems. He claims that:

> The motivation for creating a school subject that focuses on technology as a discipline and as a phenomenon in our culture has been for most countries that (future) citizens ought to have a good concept of what technology is and the skills to deal with it effectively. The importance of this is, in the first place, that it will enable them to live in a modern society in which technology has come to play such a vital role. "Living" in this respect means more than surviving. They ought to have control over technology rather than vice versa (de Vries 2000, 911).

These aims are difficult to achieve. One of the difficulties concerns the general issue of value education. How could, or should, one try to handle values in school; for instance, regarding the problem of control over technology? Another difficulty arises if policy makers wish to integrate technology education with other goals of education, such as equity or environmental sustainability. Interdisciplinary education and problem-centered teaching are highly complex endeavors. Technology education might be treated as a separate curricular theme, losing out on opportunities to integrate technology knowledge and skills, for instance, with environmental issues. Such a holistic approach is the main message of this book. Policy-making must show sensitivity to this integration.

Moreover, in a globalized economy, technology education should be kept up-to-date in terms of developments in industry and science, while emphasizing their social, ethical, and cultural implications. STS educational programs (Science, Technology, and Society) attempt to fulfill this role. For instance, the Israeli science curriculum for junior high schools focuses on the impact of scientific and technological developments, such as in vitro fertilization; on society; and on such developments' links with cultural norms. De Vries (2000, 917, italics added) mentions several basic conditions for technology education:

- The availability of well-trained *teachers*.
- The availability of sufficient and adequate *facilities* (including teaching and learning *materials*).
- Education *research* to support the further development of technology education.
- *International co-operation* to enable countries to gain from each other's experiences.

This list represents the three main domains of technology education that are essential for policy-making and international cooperation: curricula, teaching, and teacher education. These three domains are treated in depth in part II of this book. But here it should be emphasized that even the best curricular programs for technology education are only as good as the willingness, knowledge, and skills of the teachers who implement them. Thus, teacher education programs must include special courses and experiences for teachers in multiple aspects of technology.

For students to achieve a high level of critical and reflective learning, their teachers must act as mentors. Teacher education programs play a crucial role in this endeavor. Chronaki (2000, 565) suggests four different "avenues" that influence the nature of pedagogy in classrooms using computers:

- The *pedagogical orientation* of the macrolevel educational system where the computer is implemented. Some systems embrace the wide use of computers and devote substantial funding to this endeavor, whereas in other systems, digital education is minimal.
- The *pedagogical structure* (namely, software programs) embedded within the computer system. Appropriate programs are relatively rare.
- The *pedagogical organization* of the classroom lessons. Teachers might rely completely on the computer program as a self-contained unit, without integrating it with other instructional strategies, such as classroom discussion.
- The *pedagogical support* that teachers provide while intervening in students' activities. This kind of support depends on teachers' ability to ascertain students' needs.

Policy-making must relate to these avenues in order to ensure successful uses of computerized technologies.

With regard to learners, policy makers cannot ignore the information:

The learner is no longer seen as a passive recipient of information (or the consumer of prescriptive guidelines) but has the potential actively to interact with information technology tools and peers and to construct meaning via exploration, discovery, trial and error, and social engagement (Chronaki 2000, 560).

This view of learners is congruent with the escalating present-day trends toward self-regulatory (Zimmerman 2002), constructivist (Richardson 2003), and student-centered (Pedersen and Liu 2003) approaches to teaching and learning.

As a result of the communication networks afforded by technology today, an exciting new form of learning with computers concerns collaboration opportunities among students within schools, between schools, or even cross-nationally. Such collaborative activities, like interactive forums, organized cross-school problem solving via the web, or e-learning, are especially meaningful for learning about the environment or for getting to know diverse cultures.

CONCLUDING COMMENTS

Technology and information technology advance at a mind-boggling speed. Communication has never been easier, and the dynamics of the information superhighway have changed many aspects of human life. These developments pose grave problems for education, which strives to enable future citizens to live in modern society while having control over technology rather than being ruled by it.

Inasmuch as "technology education lacks a clear definition and a clearly defined knowledge base" (Gibson 2008, 3), any attempt to enhance student's technological capability should espouse a holistic orientation. Gibson emphasized the need to help students go beyond the mere acquisition of technological skills and to achieve "meaningful practical solutions to real problems framed within an appropriate set of values and underpinned by appropriate knowledge" (12). In other words, technology education should therefore integrate three intersecting areas—skills; problem-solving capacities such as intellectual curiosity; and a set of interpersonal and moral values—for the welfare of present populations as well as for the future.

In this context, it is important to note that these three intersecting areas—skills, problem solving, and values—could play a role in systemic education policy concerning all four main dimensions of global change examined in this part of the book, namely: immigration, economy, technology, and environment. The next chapter concerns environmental issues that threaten the future as a result of globalization.

4

Environmental Degradation

The rise in both world population and the consumption per head has led to pressure on the global environment of intensity unknown in human history (J. C. I. Dooge, *Policy Responses to Global Environmental Issues: An Introductory Overview*, 1996, 100).

The changing environment of our planet is conceived as threatening the very existence of the world as we know it, and this threat calls for new policy-making in education. Environmental policy-making in education, for this and future generations, is critical because accountability for the creative solutions that can eventually address crucial environmental issues lays directly at the doorstep of powerful decision makers who themselves have studied in the educational system and who have children in the educational system. Most probably, those individuals who will make the most momentous of future decisions regarding the fate of our planet are still children now in the current educational system and can even yet be influenced by policy makers of today.

The environmental pressure on Earth is expressed in manifold physical ways: global warming; ozone depletion; the rise in pollution of air and water; depletion of natural resources such as oil and minerals; desertification; possible worldwide transmission of diseases; and more. However, as Caldwell (2005, 147) states: "The question of mankind's ability to protect the biosphere is a multiple question of understandings, values, priorities, and their behavioral consequences—not primarily of technical possibilities." An interplay of ethical, geopolitical, economic, and social considerations appears to influence the decision makers who could potentially slow down or halt the destructive trajectory of current environmental processes.

"Political instability, ignorance, avarice, rapid population growth, disorder, and violence are deterrents to all aspects of environmental protection" (Caldwell 2005, 148).

As far back as the 1970s and 1980s, profound worldwide concern emerged regarding environmental problems. The hasty development of industries in western states has raised concerns regarding topics such as air pollution, toxicology of dangerous gases, pesticides, and nature reserves. In addition, the massive establishment of urban centers has created a population movement from rural to urban areas and the formation of numerous cities, thereby narrowing the amount of nature reserves and increasing air pollution.

Several international conferences have addressed a broad range of environmental problems. Among these are the Stockholm Conference in 1972 and the United Nations Conference on Environment and Development in Rio de Janeiro in 1992, as well as the more recent Bali Climate Change Conference in 2007. These conferences helped identify a "roadmap" for international policy and action for the twenty-first century. The main results of such international cooperation have been investigations undertaken to isolate the causes of environmental problems.

Environmental studies attempt to address the problem from an academic point of view. They deal with the complex issues of the relationships between human beings and the environment, addressing both the philosophical and practical aspects of the matter. Public organizations, governments, municipalities, and industrial institutions are also operating in an attempt to properly address the environmental problem. Nonetheless, little actual progress has been noted on the ground:

> Governments have found it easier to sign declarations and to collaborate in joint scientific investigations such as the International Geophysical Year, the International Indian Ocean Expedition, and the Global Atmospheric Research Programme than to fulfill environmental agreements through regulatory measures of their own, or through conformity to international policies or standards (Caldwell 2005, 147).

Caldwell goes on to declare that "environmentally concerned people and their governments face a task as difficult as humans ever face—the changing of human behavior" (147). The complex range of human attitudes and behaviors embedded in culture account for the ways in which humanity impacts the environment, and these are decidedly resistant to change.

It is highly questionable whether coercion and regulations are going to solve environmental problems as long as immediate personal, social, or national interests govern the behavior of people. The prospects are discouraging, but humanity does not have a choice. People must face these problems in order to direct the world into a sustainable future. Hence, it seems that a real change can only be brought about by education. Unless these academic and political attempts are complemented by the education of environmentally aware citizens, the aim of protecting the environment cannot be achieved.

The possible impact of environmental degradation has moral and political implications with far-reaching consequences for policy-making in education. McCloskey (1983) analyzes some of the claims made about environmental degradation and the possibility of an ensuing "ecological crisis." According to McCloskey, different writers have emphasized different elements as constituting this crisis: resource depletion, population size and growth, pollution, endangerment of species, and loss of wilderness. "Much of the concern expressed by ecological moralists is for human survival and the quality of life human beings will enjoy if they survive. A moral concern also is expressed by many, however, for the well-being of the earth's ecosystem, and its living members and inanimate components" (McCloskey 1983, 6).

With regard to expectations for future crises, McCloskey differentiates between the projection of present-day trends into the future and predictions based on sound scientific foundations, boldly stating: "Most of the predictions of an ecological crisis lack a sound scientific basis. They rest not at all on the findings of the science of ecology and are ecological only in that the ecological interactions of the various factors contributing to the crisis are stressed by those who make such a prediction" (McCloskey 1983, 15). According to McCloskey, computer outputs cannot be considered predictions, as the real world is not expected to adhere to theoretical modes.

McCloskey's book was written in 1983, and it may be unclear twenty-five years later whether the ecological crisis has already arrived or still lies in the future. In either case, important, philosophically interesting, and practical issues of ecological ethics and politics are at stake. McCloskey presents the view of some ecological moral philosophers who argue:

> Our duties in respect of nature, the preservation of species, wilderness, and natural phenomena, relate both to the case for retaining actual and possible future resources as renewable resources, and also to the question of whether nature and its constituents should morally be respected for their own sakes (McCloskey 1983, 7).

These various moral issues raised by McCloskey have considerable implications for any policy-making in education that strives for moral legitimacy.

Yet, policy-making must be politically feasible and cannot be left to the goodwill or admirable intentions of individuals, whatever positions of power or influence they may hold. Political solutions and political actions are a necessity. Political action is far from easy when it comes to issues such as conservation of resources, prevention of pollution, or the preservation of species and natural phenomena. Even as far back as 1983, McCloskey claimed that such political action ". . . must necessarily involve the curtailment of the freedom of persons, their self-development, and their enjoyment of well-being, by means of criminal, taxation, and various other laws" (McCloskey 1983, 9).

It may well be that an urgent ecological crisis would require the response of draconic measures. The history of international action in the face of global warming, for instance, does not foretell a situation that will enable the necessary kinds of social and political arrangements. Appropriate policies of education, at all age levels, are urgently required.

DESIGNING POLICY FOR ENVIRONMENTAL EDUCATION

Environmental education aims at producing citizens who use their environment rationally in order to develop the highest quality of life for all, who are knowledgeable about the environment and act responsibly, and who make appropriate decisions based on rational considerations (Ben-Peretz 1980). Environmental education should be comprehensive and integrative, aiming at all citizens. The goal of education in schools, at home, and through youth movements is to create communities that behave responsibly toward the environment. Major education efforts must focus on promoting the enlightenment of citizens regarding the urgency of environmental issues and gaining citizens' commitment to changing their own destructive behavior.

The integrative nature of environmental education may be manifested in several ways. First, being a complex issue, environmental education should include topics from various disciplines. Environmental problems entail many aspects. Therefore, environmental education must include the biological, social, economic, cultural, ethical, and aesthetic components of the environment. Environmental policy should integrate science with law, engineering, political science, and other relevant disciplines. Second, environmental education should use research and scientific data while addressing the topic. Third, environmental education should include the activities of schools, other institutions, and people in the community.

What policies of education might promote these goals? One of Oulton and Scott's (2000) main claims, in their *Environmental Education: A Time for Re-Visioning*, is that environmental education tends to be theory-led and thereby problematic for practitioners in education. Learning about the physics or chemistry of air pollution or the biology of polluted streams, if devoid of any practical implications, cannot achieve the goals of environmental education, namely sustaining the environment. Practical action outside schools must be a logical conclusion to any ecologically sound curriculum. The following part of this chapter presents some of their arguments, which altogether support a call for a holistic approach to policy (proposed later in the book), which can appropriately address the complex systemic issues confronting education in global times.

Oulton and Scott (2000, 490) present a list of requirements for environmental education in any setting:

- Recognition of a shared, community-based environmental problem, which is solvable by school students
- School and parental agreement that the environmental problem will become the focus of the curriculum
- Committed teachers, school principal, and community
- Preparedness on behalf of the teachers, students, and community participants to confront their own values and the values held by others
- A teacher with specific expertise in relation to the problem, or an outside expert

According to Oulton and Scott, a basic weakness in curricular programs that are limited in scope or time, treating only specific issues such as recycling or global warming for a small number of lessons, is that they lack an appropriate conceptual framework and practical principles for implementation. The addition of a theoretical framework and its corollary principles might help practitioners adjust such curricular programs to their own specific environmental situations, with the aim of achieving practical local results. For example, learning about the issue of global warming could be based on theories in physics, geography, or biology, including some principals for action derived from these theories.

A change in the curriculum seems to be an important step forward in effectively integrating environmental education into the school system. Two different integrative policy approaches have been suggested. One calls for special environmental programs that draw upon traditionally relevant disciplines, such as biology and chemistry. The other approach, advocated by Brennan (1974), calls for appropriately incorporating environmental aspects into each of the traditional disciplines.

Brennan claims that in order to be successful and enduring, programs must not be narrowly conceived but rather must become an integral part of general education. Specially designed integrative curricula, with emphasis on environmental issues, have already been introduced in several U.S. states as far back as the 1970s. Both approaches advocate integrated science and can thus help students gain an understanding of the function of science in everyday life. In addition, both approaches can be used to include both global and local concerns about environmental issues. Even when dealing with global issues, meaningful environmental education should manifest itself in activities and problems that are relevant to a specific community or region.

Lucas (1979) distinguishes among education about, in, and for the environment. Education "about" the environment concerns facts and theories about planet Earth. Education "in" the environment may be viewed as using the physical surroundings as a medium for teaching and learning. Finally, education "for" the environment involves teaching the students modes for critically interacting with the environment in order to sustain and improve it. According to Oulton and Scott: "Education *for* the environment has become synonymous with environmental education" (2000, 492, italics added).

Environmental education is assumed to lead to actions that conserve and improve the environment. This is its raison d'être, yet this also constitutes its inherent weakness. Educational endeavors are generally school-based and do not include active involvement in civic action, therefore the requirements of environmental education are unique and problematic for the school system.

> Action competence is a set of capabilities which equip individuals with the ability to act in whatever way they choose: actions are not predetermined, as with behavior-chance strategies, but are commensurate with the liberal democratic goals of environmental education as set out, for example, in the Tbilisi Declaration (UNESCO-UNEP 1978). . . . Actions must be judged in relation to their educational value (Oulton and Scott 2000, 495).

This emphasis on "action competence" as a central goal of environmental education is close to Schwab's (1983) definition of curriculum. Curriculum according to Schwab concerns, among other things, the aims of promoting in students "a propensity to act and react" (240). Thus, curriculum is viewed as a vehicle not only for transmitting knowledge but also for promoting the actual abilities of future citizens to act and react in appropriate ways to social and environmental problems. A concrete example of a curriculum endeavor confronting one environmental problem is the booklet on global warming that is described next.

CASE ILLUSTRATION: CURRICULUM MATERIALS CONFRONTING ENVIRONMENTAL ISSUES

The topic of global warming may be an excellent case for introducing students to environmental issues because it is prevalent in media reports. After a brief presentation of this special case, this section offers comments on the possible integration of this case into other dimensions of global change.

The booklet for teachers *Teaching about Climate Change* (Grant and Little-john 2001) aims to introduce students of different ages to the issues of climate change. The main goal of this curriculum material is to encourage teachers and students "to take action on climate change" (1). The authors claim that ". . . climate change is a phenomenon with which we humans have little experience, at least in historic times, and teaching about it presents special challenges to educators" (1). Educators find themselves up ". . . against the ingrained habits and attitudes of an industrial society created and powered by fossil fuel and supported by political inertia in establishing regulatory policies to curb greenhouse gas emission" (1).

The booklet provides some information about climate change and about several international attempts to work together to prevent dangerous interference with the climate system. In view of the seeming unwillingness of governments and industries to implement binding regulations to reduce greenhouse gas emissions, the authors argue that schools have the advantage of combining conservation strategies with education programs that link lifestyle choices to environmental sustainability. Curricula in science, social studies, geography, health, and other disciplines are viewed as offering a plethora of opportunities to introduce students to issues of climate change. For example, McClaren and Hammond (2001, 5–6) recommend five fundamental concepts in teaching about climate change that promote students' critical skills and knowledge:

- Change is the norm in the Earth's natural systems.
- The Earth's systems are linked in complex interactions.
- Global changes affect all life.
- Local, regional, and global changes are often linked.
- Humans have become major agents in global change.

In Grant and Littlejohn's climate change booklet, diverse activities are suggested for exploring key concepts and for understanding climate phenomena. The emphasis is on implications for actions and environmental choices, like solar box cooking or organizing transportation alternatives to private cars on the drive to and from school (walking, cycling, school bus). Another important feature of this curriculum material concerns its viable suggestions for including science, language arts, math, geography, and art in the actual teaching-learning process.

Implementation of the climate change materials requires considerable commitment, knowledge, and ability among teachers. Thus, policy on environmental education should address all three major domains of education: curriculum, teaching, and teacher education. Curriculum planning that does not concurrently consider teaching modes and teacher education may confront serious problems during the implementation process. With regard to teaching, the field of environmental studies can support, and be supported by, the growing pedagogical movement toward problem solving and toward authentic and meaningful learning. For teachers to become aware of environmental problems and educate students to solve problems in their authentic environment, specialized teacher education is needed. The integrative approach to environmental education also calls for educating all teachers about the environment regardless of their subject specialization. In addition, inasmuch as environmental education is also expected to account for local, not only global, problems, teachers should be taught how to design parts of the curriculum on their own.

GENERALIZING THIS CASE TO OTHERS

All five of the main issues highlighted above are not only relevant to the specific case of climate change but may also be extended to policy-making in response to all of the interdependent dimensions of global change. Likewise, this booklet's activities, guidelines, and suggestions can all be generalized to serve as a framework for educational efforts responding to other environmental degradation changes and even to other global changes in demographics, economics, and information technology. The climate change material includes topics like energy consumption or transportation that are closely linked to demographic change. These links could be made explicit in the materials. Technological developments and global economic trends are other dimensions of globalization that could be integrated with the discussion of global warming. Similarly, climate changes may be linked to population growth and movements. Human industry and agriculture interact with energy cycles in nature and climate changes. As the authors of this material conclude: "There is good news and bad news about education that addressed global climate change. The bad news is that the topic is complex and challenging. The good news is also that it is complex and challenging" (McClaren and Hammond 2001, 8)

As stated in the Introduction chapter to the present book, one of the drawbacks of policy-making in education is its division into separate areas to account for the four globalization dimensions: environmental education, education of immigrants, technology in education, and education for global economic factors. In line with Oulton and Scott's (2000) advocacy of a multiparadigmatic and cross-disciplinary approach to education about globalization, the holistic approach proposed in this book assumes that defensible and feasible policy in education requires integration and coordination among these areas.

There is an obvious problem in trying to introduce too many topics and issues at once. Optimally, all four dimensions of global changes—

demography, economy, technology, and environment—should be integrated into the policy-making process, but not necessarily into each set of curriculum materials. Nevertheless, for each case, teachers can indicate that Earth's systems are linked in highly complex interactions; that humans are important agents in causing both negative and positive global processes; and that people are ultimately responsible for their own responses to calls for change.

CONCLUDING COMMENTS

This chapter focuses on the crucial problem of environmental degradation, showing that in spite of growing awareness of these issues, very little has actually been done globally. Education alone cannot be held responsible for responding to environmental problems, but it can play a role in raising the consciousness of present and future citizens, motivating them to act and react to these problems. Part II leads us to a discussion of three major domains of education systems that must take on an active involvement in this endeavor: curricula, teaching, and teacher education.

II

THE MAGIC NUMBER "3": COORDINATING THREE DOMAINS OF EDUCATION IN RESPONSE TO GLOBALIZATION

PART II INTRODUCTION

The first part of this book has briefly presented some of the major global changes characterizing today's world. Some of the implications for education posed by each of these changes were discussed.

The Delors Report (1996) states the following goals for education agendas in the coming decades: learning to be, learning to know, learning to do, and learning to live together. These goals cover essential aspects of education: identity formation, gaining knowledge, mastery of practical skills, and the highly important cultivation of interpersonal relationships, meaning person-to-person relationships but also responsibility for the community as a whole. This second part of the book presents some literature in education that holds implications for achieving these goals in responding to global changes.

The systemic approach to policy-making adapted in the current book coordinates three central domains of education. It seems that human beings generally tend to divide phenomena into sets of threes. For example, a Jewish saying states that "the world stands on account of three things: study of God's words, divine worship, and acts of kindness" (Ethics of our Fathers, 1:2). There is also, for instance, the well-known division of classroom situations into three parts as well: the teacher, the student, and the subject matter. In the current volume, however, the "magical" three domains of education comprise curriculum, teachers' roles, and teacher education.

Goodlad et al.'s (1979) view of the various phases of the curriculum enterprise conceives teachers as the main actors in classroom events, perceiving, planning, and implementing curriculum materials. Much has been written about teachers' crucial roles in curriculum as interpreters, adaptors, and creators of curricula (Ben-Peretz 1990a; Connelly and Clandinin 1988).

Yet, there is a missing link in this sequence, leading from curricula developers to classroom use. This missing link concerns the function of teacher education programs to enable teachers to fulfill their roles in the curriculum enterprise. Research on teacher education treats many important components of teacher education programs but is mostly silent on the preparation of teachers as curriculum implementers and planners (Cochran-Smith and Zeichner 2005). Policy-making in education cannot ignore the centrality of teacher education in the process of bridging between policy intentions and the realities of classroom practice.

CASE ILLUSTRATION: ISRAELI JUNIOR HIGH SCHOOLS

The case of structural educational reform (described in detail below in chapter 10) provides an example in the Israeli context of the three-way interrelations to be discussed here in this part of the present book—among curricula, teachers' roles, and teacher education. Sometimes changes in all three of these domains arise as outcomes of structural policy innovation.

As seen below in the following chapter (and in chapter 10), the Israeli school reform in the 1970s started with a structural metamorphosis of the educational system, from a design comprising eight years of elementary schooling followed by four years of high school to a structure comprising six years (elementary) + three years (junior high) + three years (senior high) of schooling.

The Israeli creation of separate junior high schools was accompanied by new expectations from teachers and required the development of appropriate curricula and congruent changes in teacher education. A special department for curriculum development was formed in the Ministry of Education and was specifically assigned the task of preparing curricula for these new junior high schools. Moreover, a new mode of teacher education ensued. Teacher education underwent a process of academization: One year of required studies was added to the previously three-year teacher educator program, leading to a four-year BEd program.

This example reflects the ecological interdependence of curriculum, teachers' roles, and teacher education in educational policy. It is contended, herewith, that policy-making in response to global changes must coordinate these three major domains of education: curriculum development, the practice of teaching, and teacher education. Ignoring any one of these domains leads to a disruption of the organic chain leading from curricula that target global concerns to expected teachers' practice in schools. My own series of research studies over the years systematically targeted all of the domains.

Part II of this book presents a selection of my writings on these three major domains, as well as the works of others, while interrelating the three domains and analyzing their implications for policy-making. Each chapter begins with a brief discussion of the relations among the domains and their overall meaning for policy-making as a systemic response to global changes.

5

The Curriculum Domain and Policy-Making in Education

As described in some detail in the first part of this book, global changes echo widely in the education system, calling for adaptation to pressing global concerns and issues. Curriculum and curriculum development cannot be detached from the social, cultural, and political contexts, both at local and international levels. Therefore, educational curricula must be developed while maintaining deep sensitivity to these contexts. In Israel, an examination of curriculum development, as it has evolved over time, reveals that policy makers have reacted to significant globalization issues such as immigration and demographic changes, the ensuing socioeconomic gaps between different communities within Israeli society, and environmental issues.

Curriculum development is also strongly connected to ideology movements. Due to ideology's cardinal role in policy-making, a discussion of curriculum and ideology is pertinent to any attempt for policy-making to respond to global challenges.

CURRICULUM AND IDEOLOGY

An intricate relationship connects ideological changes with policies of curriculum development. Several research studies reflect this intricacy. The paper "Culture and Ideology: The Development of a National Curriculum in Israel," which was presented at the Society for the Study of Curriculum History, Culture and Ideology (Ben-Peretz 1996), for example, unfolds Israel's changing cultural and ideological contexts during the last fifty years as they have influenced the process of curriculum development, the nature of curricular materials, and curricular implementation. Earlier, Ben-Peretz and Zajdman (1986) identified three different periods of change in Israeli curriculum development: the "pre-scientific" period lasting up to the establishment of the Center for Curriculum Development in the Ministry of Education; the "scientific" period from the late 1960s till the early 1980s, when curriculum development was centralized; and the "open" period, since the 1980s, when school-based curriculum development became an acceptable and even desirable alternative.

REVISITING THE CASE OF STRUCTURAL REFORM

The case illustration of structural reform mentioned in the introduction to this part of the book offers an opportunity to relate to the close link between policy and curriculum and to examine several aspects of curriculum development in Israel: the ideological and practical rationale underlying policy makers' initiation of the reform, the chronological changes typifying Israeli curriculum development, and the dilemmas they faced.

During the 1960s and 1970s, Israel experienced a massive educational reform as a result of both ideology related to the perceived educational needs in a changing society as well as lessons learned from curricular developments occurring in the USA and Britain. As noted above, this structural reform entailed the establishment of comprehensive junior high schools for grades 7–9. The reform derived from the perceived inadequate quality of teaching and learning during the final two years of elementary school and from the high percentage of failure and dropout characterizing the postelementary stage.

The rationale for instituting junior high schools at that time connected with the vast immigration that the fledgling country had experienced since its establishment and the accompanying changes in school populations. Israeli society was, and still is, multiethnic and multicultural, including Arabs and Jews, orthodox and secular, and massive numbers of Jewish immigrants from diverse Western and Asian countries of origin. In the 1970s, the disturbing correlation between failure or low achievement and students' geocultural origin called for historic policy measures (Inbar 1981). Thus, in line with an egalitarian ideology, the junior high structural reform aimed at creating equal educational opportunities for all students to improve achievements. Concurrently, in line with a melting-pot ideology, the new reform hoped to promote social integration and homogeneity between diverse groups.

The case of structural reform also presents a historical account of how changes transpired in the accepted view of who should create, implement, and evaluate curriculum in Israel. Originally, to provide curricular guidelines and appropriate textbooks for the new policy, the Center for Curriculum Development was established as part of the national Ministry of Education. It was believed that centralized guidelines and nationally prescribed curricula would ensure the success of the new reform and that a common core curriculum would diminish gaps among student populations. However, over time, toward the 1980s and 1990s, this centrality of guidelines and materials began to come under question as being unresponsive to local needs (Eden 1991). Local authorities and the Ministry started to support school-based curriculum development (Sabar et al 1987). The evolution of the national curriculum in Israel and the slow devolution of curricular authority created major dilemmas.

One dilemma relates to the power relations between center and periphery. Up to the present day, the Israeli education system continues to be centralized and guided by the Ministry. Under these circumstances, the authentic handover of authority to local schools is questionable. Central authorities must approve even locally developed curricula, and the Ministry holds authority over educational decision-making. Tensions gradually mount between center and periphery as municipalities, parents, and teachers want to become more involved in educational planning. Although in the 1990s the Ministry advocated a new policy founded on school-based management, its success and impact on the national curriculum remain unclear (Sabar 1990; Sabar and Dushnik 1996; Sabar and Silberstein 1999).

A second dilemma that arose from changes in policies of curriculum development is related to issues of cultural heterogeneity versus social integration of immigrants who came to Israel from different countries and cultures (see chapter 1). Reflecting the melting-pot ideology, curriculum development in Israel until the late 1970s supported social integration and unification. For the first three decades of the country's existence, a common curriculum was considered the best means to promote equal opportunities and national unity.

Nonetheless, the educational establishment in Israel has always recognized the needs and richness of a highly diverse society. Various sectors in society were able to incorporate their own unique components into the national curriculum, and even to develop their own curriculum, as in the religiously observant Jewish or Arab schools.

Yet, beyond these sectors, over time, a change has undeniably transpired in Israeli curricula that reflects new attitudes toward the role of education in society in general. The emerging voices of cultural and societal minority groups found their way into the accepted ideology of policy makers, and the Israeli curriculum started to mirror the heterogeneous multiculturalism of its population. The curriculum in history and literature became varied according to different geocultural viewpoints. Schools introduced learning activities that celebrated diversity.

Nowadays, the curriculum endeavors to maintain a balance between commonalities and solidarity on the one hand and uniqueness and diversity on the other hand. However, this balance presents a difficult challenge for teachers and policy makers alike. The following vignette taken from Ben-Peretz and Kupferberg (2007) exemplifies an inexperienced teacher's difficulties posed by classroom heterogeneity:

> My problem is that I simply don't manage to respond to the entire broad range of levels in every class. I don't find the time to plan every lesson so that it suits the 3rd and the 4th grades as well as at least some of the special needs of some of the children in each class. I know that this is a problem that many teachers have, and I don't want to "whine," but my time has simply become the most valuable resource. I'm torn between my family (I have the sweetest three-year-old daughter who is naturally my first priority), my studies and my work. And the most frustrating thing is that even when I've finally managed to find the time to sit at home and plan 5–6 separate activities for each lesson, in the end I don't succeed in doing them in class at all. I don't know if there is a solution to this situation. It's probably not a simple solution (134).

Teacher education must play a major role in preparing teachers to use curricular materials in ways that respond to heterogeneous classrooms and cultural diversity.

CURRICULA FOR THE FUTURE

Curricular decisions possess a moral nature. The school curriculum should be based upon a view of the future citizens. How do educators envision that students will form their identities, interact with others, and act on their choices? The goal is obviously for those students to become mature and fulfilled individuals who forge meaningful relationships with other human beings, commit to significant work that contributes to the betterment of our world, and proactively uphold a sense of social responsibility. This notion is vital to ensure that the students of today become future adults who can make moral and responsible choices about the environment, the world economy, the uses of modern technology, and the changing nature of the population.

We move now from a brief historical overview of curriculum changes in response to societal and ideological changes in one country to a general discussion of this issue based on an essay reviewing Beyer and Liston's 1996 book, *Curriculum in Conflict: Social Visions, Educational Agendas, and Progressive School Reform.*

"THE QUEST FOR UTOPIA: SOCIAL IDEOLOGIES AND THE CURRICULUM" (BEN-PERETZ 1997)

Research studies investigating the intricate relationships between educational endeavors and social ideologies may be highly relevant to policy-making in response to global changes. To a large extent, social ideologies and social trends may determine the construction and implementation of school curricula. The Beyer and Liston book offers insights into how the social currents and ideologies characterizing specific surroundings often intertwine with curricula and curricular practice. Beyer and Liston assert that a deep understanding of these ties is crucial in order to construct public-school-system curricula.

Curricula and Utopia

Beyer and Liston argue that the curriculum field is one of the most promising domains for developing appropriate means and ends for education. They further assume that curricula serve as a means for avoiding perceived social dangers or for supporting certain social initiatives. The book's central statement claims that "curriculum design is a form of 'utopianism'" (MacDonald 1975; cited in Beyer and Liston 1996, xvi), a desire to change the world for the better following certain theories and ideologies.

Beyer and Liston's book asserts that inasmuch as curricula are geared to preparing students for their future, the curriculum's type, quality, and distribution of knowledge are influenced by assumptions about those students' possible futures. These assumptions were demonstrated in Anyon's (1981) research, which showed how students' and teachers' perceived future occupation and social class determined the curriculum that students experienced in schools serving different social classes. Whatever the grand curriculum design and its relation to different ideologies might be, the center of the educational stage will always include the present, lived-in curriculum in the classroom.

The discussion about democratic values and processes lies at the center of Beyer and Liston's book, which attempts to portray a holistic view of the development of social theory and how it shapes educational practice. The community's shared concerns about educational planning constitute a vital component in the current book's approach to policy-making, as reflected in part IV below. A major claim of this agenda is that the possibilities offered by education in a democracy expand when that democracy is viewed as a shared way of life, when learning is seen as involving people who are engaged in experiences within which they can grow, and when community is considered a central part of life.

One way of translating this view into the educational context uses what Nicholson calls "a rainbow coalition" (1989, 204), which includes educators who are committed to integrating voices into the talk that shapes curriculum and civilization. According to this notion, curriculum deliberations should always include the social, political, and cultural contexts in which they are embedded. Likewise, knowledge and understanding should be tied inherently into the world of action. Students' interventions in their physical environment, in their economic, political, or cultural practice, comprise an important aspect of curricular planning. The policy-making model presented later in the present book adopts the view of a "rainbow coalition" as the necessary basis for policy-making in education.

Curriculum is the major element by which an educational policy is expressed in the practice of education. Thus, defining curriculum use and understanding the ways in which curricula are implemented could assist policy planners in forming a practical and relevant policy. The following section, which is based on a recent chapter, "Curriculum Use in the Classroom" (Ben-Peretz and Eilam, in press), reflects this issue.

USING CURRICULUM IN CLASSROOMS

Curriculum use may be defined as how curricular materials are applied, utilized, handled, and possibly even manipulated by different educational agents or stakeholders. Materials may include teacher handbooks or guidelines, syllabi, textbooks, additional instructional materials, and materials for student assessment. The use of those curricular materials entails an interaction among three stakeholders—teachers, learners, and society. As can be seen from the following discussion of these stakeholders, they become central agents in implementing and using curriculum.

The Teacher as a Stakeholder and Agent in Curriculum Use

Examining the modes in which teachers use curriculum, research conducted in the 1980s identified several different modes. One mode is for teachers to act as users of teacher-proof curriculum; that is, they are expected to use the curriculum exactly as prescribed. A second way is when teachers act as choice makers, coming to their own decisions about uses of materials. Third, teachers can be curriculum adaptors, changing the curriculum materials to fit their interests and knowledge or their perceptions about students' needs (Ben-Peretz 1990a).

A fourth mode of teacher involvement in the curriculum endeavor occurs when teachers create their own curricular materials, based on general policy guidelines. By using their imagination, teachers thus gain ownership of the curriculum. Such a decentralized mode of teacher involvement has several advantages, providing individualized curriculum materials for students with special needs or developing courses in response to local societal problems. Here, teachers' use of the curriculum is influenced by their beliefs (Fullan 1982), personal factors (Miller and Seller 1985), and the interactive process between the curriculum materials and their own educational contexts.

Teachers' classroom experiences while implementing the curriculum can reduce the ambiguity that often characterizes curriculum planners' stated intentions. The concrete experiences created by actual curriculum implementation might correspond with the planners' perceived intentions, but then again might also differ from them, enacting the implicit "curriculum potential" (Ben-Peretz 1990a). The notion of "curriculum potential" emerges from the interaction between teachers and materials. Teachers can develop their own curricular ideas based on the given materials, using their own insights, pedagogical knowledge, and professional imagination. Forming a relevant curriculum should take into account teachers' insights and viewpoints as well as offer "potential" for diverse educational situations. The subject of curriculum potential is further elaborated later in this chapter.

The Learner as a Stakeholder and Agent in Curriculum Use

The curriculum as experienced by learners is one of the most critical phases in the curriculum transformation model suggested by Goodlad, Klein, and Tye (1979). Their model tracks five phases of curriculum interpretation, ranging from the ideological curriculum in the eyes of its creators, to the formal, approved curriculum, to the curriculum perceived in the teachers' minds, to the curriculum enacted by the teachers, and finally to learners' actual experiences with the enacted curriculum.

To evaluate how students experience a curriculum, researchers can measure the students' achievements or conduct observations of the interaction between students and the curriculum materials. The classroom context often determines how students use a curriculum; for example, learners' interpretation of the meaning of a text may be affected by their classroom's social context or by broader psychosocial variables such as gender, social class, personality, and ethnicity (Kalmus 2004).

One of the ways in which students interact with the curriculum is by participating in a community of discourse, where students and teachers share their knowledge and experiences. Such a constructive classroom environment enables students to act as "teachers" and "leaders," thus actively engaging in curriculum use. As the classroom teachers seek to increase their understanding of their students' conceptions regarding the material being studied, the learners naturally and gradually take on the role of planners for their own curriculum use.

Society as a Stakeholder and Agent in Curriculum Use

Society as a stakeholder includes parents, policy makers, diverse societal groups, and other members of society outside the classroom. Almost any curriculum can be utilized for achieving societal goals and agendas, which change across time and social context. For instance, teachers can use curriculum materials in mathematics to eliminate gender differences in achievement. Curriculum materials in history may serve agendas of multiculturalism and equity. An example of a science curriculum fostering societal goals is the response of educators in the United States to the competition in space technology with the Soviet Union.

Society and culture affect the use of curriculum in classrooms in terms of both contents and goals. For instance, because of immigration and demographic changes in the classroom composition, students' diversity may impact the scope and content of curriculum use in the classroom, such as in language teaching, which may become more complex and require expansion (Sowell 2000). Society has also long been viewed as one of the sources of curriculum objectives (Hlebowitsh 1999). As far back as the 1940s, Tyler saw curriculum as serving societal needs. Later, inasmuch as the perception of "society" began to shift from that of a single uniform entity to that of an amalgamation of groups and individuals, curriculum scholars starting in the 1960s called for a reconceptualization of curriculum theories to account for their simultaneously beneficial and harmful effects on different social subgroups (Anyon 1981). Curricula are viewed as political texts (Apple et al. 2007) that serve political goals of policy makers. Even when not serving explicit societal purposes of keeping the status quo, curriculum implementation transmits societal expectations, as shown in the Anyon study.

Apart from being viewed as a political text, curriculum might also be regarded as an economic text. In response to globalization tendencies, today's societal agendas are shifting to adjust to the rapid pace of economical and technological changes. As discussed in chapter 3, instrumental trends in curriculum are now being used to achieve the social goals of preparing students for labor in the current globalization and technological age. Inasmuch as global competition is causing a rise in standards of efficiency and productivity, various countries have already formed committees to adapt their national educational goals to face these changes (Bishop 1990; Smith III 1999). Nonetheless, the debate over issues of preparing students for the changing demands of workplaces continues. Some researchers have suggested that the relations between education and workplace productivity are complex (Smith III 1999) or unnecessary altogether (Bishop 1990).

In sum, policy makers in education should account for the three users of curriculum discussed by Ben-Peretz and Eilam (in press) in two ways: one, as stakeholders whose interests have to be considered, and two, as crucial agents of curriculum implementation and use.

FURTHER INTERACTIONS RELATED TO CURRICULUM USE IN THE CLASSROOM

Remillard's (1999) article, "Curriculum Materials in Mathematics Education Reform: A Framework for Examining Teachers' Curriculum Development," sheds light on teachers as curriculum users and developers and on curriculum use in general. Remillard examined two experienced teachers' interactions with a new mathematics textbook in order to understand how curriculum materials might foster changes in teaching mathematics. Her research suggests that the actual curriculum enacted in the classroom results from interactions between teachers' professional beliefs and goals, the written materials, and their students' needs and performances. This finding supports the integrative approach to policy-making presented in the present book, as it ties curriculum planning in with actual teaching and bears implications for teacher education. Teachers need to be introduced into the different modes of curriculum use, as choice makers, adaptors, and creators of curriculum. The notion of "curriculum potential" is especially meaningful in this endeavor.

CURRICULUM POTENTIAL

Teachers' work in relation to planning and teaching can be regarded as curriculum development—"the processes by which teachers develop curricular plans and ideals and translate them into classroom events" (Remillard 1999, 318). Through these processes, teachers shape students' classroom experiences. Two levels of curriculum development might be conceived: curriculum writers' actions while conceptualizing curricular plans and teachers' actions while they alter, adapt, or translate textbook offerings so that they become appropriate for their students. Teachers' role as curriculum developers thus occurs on two levels, including not only the selection and redesign of curriculum plans but also the enactment of those plans with their students (Ben-Peretz 1990a).

As elaborated in *The Teacher-Curriculum Encounter: Freeing Teachers from the Tyranny of Texts* (Ben-Peretz 1990a), curriculum materials embody "curriculum potential"—namely, intended and unintended uses of the curriculum. In the process of transforming knowledge into teachable and learnable forms, the developers consider the educational potential implicit in the nature of the subject matter and its major concepts. The educational potential perceived by curriculum developers is reflected in their stated intentions and in the prepared materials (Schwab 1973).

However, the fact that curriculum materials, and, to a large extent, the curriculum itself, can be interpreted, developed, redesigned, and enacted in multiple ways suggests that curricula are not neutral or unambiguous. Research has underscored the many transformations that occur, from the original intentions of the curriculum developers to the enacted material in the classroom (Goodlad et al. 1979). While enacting curriculum materials, teachers frequently do so in ways that differ from the planners' recommended teaching modes and explicit intentions, thus leading to outcomes unintended by the curriculum developers.

An interaction between teachers and materials reveals the inherent curriculum potential. The visibility of the curriculum potential depends not only on the qualities of the materials themselves but also on teachers' interpretive abilities and professional imagination. Teachers must demonstrate the ability to recognize and extract the curriculum potential and also must be able to realistically evaluate their teaching context. In other words, a teacher's interpretations of textbooks and accompanying guidelines are influenced by how that particular teacher in that specific classroom context reads the given materials and considers how to implement them in his or her own reality.

"Reality," in this sense, encompasses not only the characteristics of a specific classroom—its size, disposition, and societal context—but also the students' backgrounds, interests, prior knowledge, conceptions, and misconceptions. Reality also includes the constraints and limitations of available resources for teachers. Time, for instance, is often perceived by teachers as the most limiting factor in their ability to fulfill the potential of curriculum materials. Teachers' beliefs and prior knowledge, among other factors, also figure into task selection. Thus, altogether, it may be said that the materials serve as a starting point, but teachers must use their insights, pedagogical knowledge, and professional mind's eye to develop their own ideas based on the given texts, illustrations, recommendations, and their student and classroom context.

The main process of teachers' interpretation is the transformation of curriculum materials into adaptive and pedagogically effective forms (Shulman 1987). The role of teachers as interpreters of curriculum materials— who search for new ways to teach and learn materials and discover new educational possibilities—is congruent with what Connelly (1972) calls teachers' roles as "users-developers." According to Connelly, even when implementing a prestructured curriculum, teachers serve as curriculum developers: they choose and modify curriculum materials to ensure their adaptation to the specific classroom situations at hand. Thus, developers and teachers might be seen as joining forces in that the characteristics and needs of actual classrooms should be the main factors in planning a curriculum (Connelly 1972).

The process of external curriculum development might be called "the first level of curriculum planning," which transforms content knowledge into teachable forms. The process of transforming curricular materials into actual learning experiences by teachers might be called the "second level of curriculum planning" (Ben-Peretz and Silberstein 1982). At both levels, decisions are made regarding content, instructional strategies, and the teaching context. External developers' and user-developers' previous experiences, personal knowledge, and belief systems guide many of these decisions. While the development process at the first level is convergent, ending in the creation of curriculum materials that are defined by predetermined characteristics, the process at the second level is divergent, leading to different teaching-learning settings.

The notion of two levels of curriculum development and the educational possibilities offered by the envisioned curricular potential are important considerations for policy makers, as well. At the first level, policy makers can communicate their general goals and intentions and determine the recommended scope and content of their policy. Then, at the implementation phase, local educators might transform stated general policy directives into divergent forms that are appropriate for local conditions and specific needs, thus using the potential embedded in the policy directives.

CONCLUDING COMMENTS

Several issues related to the curriculum domain are presented in this chapter, based on relevant literature. The three major curricular issues that have manifold implications for policy-making are the role of ideology in the curricular endeavor; different stakeholders and agents in curriculum use; and the notion of curriculum potential. As argued throughout this book, curriculum must be coordinated with teaching. This lies at the focus of chapter 6.

6

The Role of Teachers and Policy-Making in Education

The teacher's role in education is most complex and demands flexibility and adaptation to situational changes, both global and local, as well as to classroom settings. This complexity creates experiences that, together, form the teachers' understanding of their role. A major factor is obviously the process of teaching. This chapter reviews literature pertaining to several aspects of this process, mainly to issues of teachers' role perceptions. Teachers' role perceptions as well as their instructional strategies are essential factors in implementing new policies responding to global changes.

One of the main arguments of the present book concerns the necessity for adopting a holistic, integrated view of the educational system. According to this approach, three educational domains—curriculum, teaching, and teacher education—must be integrated within the process of policy-making. Development of curriculum materials that does not carefully consider the complexities of teaching and does not prepare teachers for the new curricula is doomed to fail. This chapter raises some teaching issues that are deeply connected to uses of curriculum materials and to teachers' role perceptions regarding this process.

When viewing the impact that teachers' role perceptions render on teachers' attitudes and behavior in the classroom while implementing curricular directives, it is important to investigate the factors influencing these perceptions. The following section deals with two studies that examined the elements involved in shaping teachers' role perceptions. The first, a paper by Ben-Peretz, Mendelson, and Kron (2003), shows the connection between teachers' role perceptions and their teaching context. The second study, conducted by Flores and Day (2006), adds the personal history of teachers as another important element to consider while attempting to comprehend the formation of teachers' role perceptions.

TEACHERS' ROLE PERCEPTIONS VIS-À-VIS WORK CONTEXTS

Ben-Peretz, Mendelson, and Kron (2003) studied the connections between teachers' work contexts and their perceptions of themselves as teachers, in *How Teachers in Different Educational Contexts View Their Roles*. The basic premises were that, first, students of all levels and contexts should have the same opportunities to develop their potential as human beings and as learners but that this does not always occur in educational reality; second, teachers play a central role in providing these opportunities through their professional activities; and, third, teachers' role perceptions are closely related to their sense of efficacy about their work with the particular students and classrooms they teach (Bandura 1977).

Hence, different teaching contexts may affect teachers' self-images of their teaching role, which, in turn, may shape their behavior and classroom practice. The importance of "images of teaching" lies in their impact on teachers' actions, as shown in Hannay's (1996) research about the difficulties that teachers face when asked to change their practices due to the persistence of their past images. Research conducted on teaching suggests that teachers' self-definition is shaped by the dynamic interactions between the teachers and the other participants in their working contexts (Berlak and Berlak 1977; Lieberman and Miller 1984; Nias 1989).

To examine differing work contexts, all sixty of the teachers who participated in the Ben-Peretz et al. study taught in vocational (nonacademic) junior high and high schools in Israel, but the participating teachers were divided equally between two separate tracks. One track leads secondary students to matriculation examinations, which is a requirement for entrance into higher education in Israel, whereas the other track focuses solely on preparation for nonacademic occupations. The students were clearly divided between these tracks according to their achievement levels, with higher achievements in the track leading to matriculation. This divergence raises doubts concerning the possibility for teachers to provide students in these schools with equal opportunities to fulfill their personal potential.

The two-track structure thus offered an opportunity to examine how the teachers' work context (divergent characteristics of students and classrooms) affected their self-images as teachers. The study intended: (a) to reveal teachers' professional images in different teaching contexts, and (b) to identify the relations between the teachers' choices of professional images and the characteristics of the classes they taught. In order for teachers to efficaciously enable students to develop and progress to their highest potential degree, it is important to uncover and understand teachers' role perceptions and the factors shaping these perceptions, which then may lead to different classroom practices.

One way of revealing teachers' perceptions of the professional self is through metaphorical images (see, for example, Beijaard et al. 2000; Inbar 1996). The Ben-Peretz et al study stimulated teachers to reveal the "metaphors they work by" through confronting teachers with visual images in the form of drawings. These images were portrayals of different occupations that might be viewed as sharing some common traits with teaching.

The seven occupations that were presented in visual images to the participating teachers were chosen because they embody some of the qualities associated with teaching. These were shopkeeper, judge, animal keeper, entertainer, orchestra conductor, puppeteer, and animal trainer. Ben-Peretz et al. (2003) describe their choice of these particular professions as follows:

> . . . the "shopkeeper" sells goods and is perceived as reflecting a transmission role in education; the "judge" is seen as representing authority, strict rules and a judgmental attitude; "animal keepers" in zoos are perceived as the embodiment of looking after a rather difficult and demanding population acting in the roles of caregivers; "entertainers" represent the role of amusers, who may make us feel happy for a short while without demanding too much effort; "conductors" determine the nature of performances and set the format and tone of the outcome, being responsible for both the group and the individuals in it; "puppeteers" . . . implies the total passivity of their puppets. Finally, "animal trainers" use behavioristic methods, including reward and punishment, in order to achieve certain behaviors, without considering the intentions and preferences of their trainees (280).

Each teacher was asked to choose the illustration of an occupation that best reflected his or her self-image as a teacher and to explain this choice. In addition, participants were asked to suggest an additional occupation that reflected their self-image as teachers, but was not in the given set of drawings, and to comment on their choices. Relations were examined between the chosen images and class achievement level.

Results indicated that choices of metaphorical images were context-related; that is, the teaching context (track) had a significant impact on teachers' images of their professional selves. Teachers of low-achieving students tended to view their role as "caring" more than as contributing to students' knowledge growth. Perhaps the lower abilities and motivation of such students, as perceived by the teachers, leads teachers to see themselves more as "'babysitters'" (Ben-Peretz et al. 2003) who solve social problems. In contrast, teachers of high-achieving students tended to view their role more as conductors, implying a perception of their role as that of leaders who work together with talented students in harmony to achieve common high-level goals.

An interesting finding was that most teachers in both tracks tended to reject a view of teaching as judgmental and controlling; they did not choose the images of judge or puppeteer. In the realities of classrooms, teachers do spend time and effort trying to control students' behavior and learning and trying to judge their achievements. Thus, a possible gap may exist between the realities of teachers' lives and their perceived images of themselves.

This research study's results call for teacher education programs to create explicit awareness of professional images, perhaps through the direct use of metaphoric pictures that vividly speak to teachers through the visual medium. In addition, student teachers should be encouraged to develop an understanding of the relationship between images and educational context as well as to evaluate the appropriateness of different role perceptions for diverse classroom situations.

TEACHERS' ROLE PERCEPTIONS VIS-À-VIS THEIR WORK CONTEXT AND PROFESSIONAL HISTORY

Another recent research study that explored factors influencing the formation of teachers' role perceptions is *Contexts which Shape and Reshape New Teachers' Identities: A Multi-Perspective Study* (Flores and Day 2006). The study observed how beginning teachers' professional identities were shaped and reshaped during their first two years of teaching. Flores and Day investigated both the professional and cultural working environments of the teachers and their personal professional history. The shaping and reshaping of identities was examined by looking at teachers' beliefs, values, and learning experiences as well as their views regarding the challenges that they face in teaching at different school settings at different stages of teaching.

Two main phases depict novice teachers' professional development (Vonk 1984): the threshold period, when new teachers experience the shock of facing full teaching responsibilities for the first time; and the period of growing into the profession, when new teachers become accepted by their pupils and colleagues. Over time, during these two phases, novice teachers begin to develop a professional identity through an ongoing and dynamic process that involves teachers' interpretations of their own values and experiences.

A constructed and consolidated sense of professional identity renders a positive emotional influence on teachers and is therefore a key factor in becoming an effective teacher. Forming and maintaining an identity involves the teachers' views both of themselves and of the contexts in which they work. The identity that is formed is influenced not only by cognitive factors but also by the emotional climate of the school and classroom. During this process of identity formation, past experiences are combined with parts of the present experience (Feiman-Nemser 2001).

The results from Flores and Day's (2006) study indicate that new teachers' professional identities are constructed, deconstructed, and reconstructed over time under the influence of their personal biographies, experiences in preservice programs, and current school settings. A powerful interaction was found between beginning teachers' personal histories and the contextual influences of their workplaces. Teachers who worked in collaborative cultures were more likely to demonstrate positive attitudes toward teaching and to have a positive professional identity. On the other hand, teachers' personal biographies play a key role in mediating between their beliefs about themselves as teachers and their professional identities. Flores and Day state "the personal experience of being a pupil, whether positive or negative, seemed to be influential in the ways in which the participants in this study viewed themselves as teachers" (224).

Both the Ben-Peretz et al (2003) and the Flores and Day (2006) studies emphasize the role of context on teaching endeavors. This close relationship has implications for policy-making, which should carefully consider the anticipated contexts for policy implementations as well as for designing policies.

One relevant aspect of teaching in regard to context concerns the role of professional memories as shaping teachers' practices.

THE IMPACT OF TEACHING SITUATIONS ON TEACHERS' MEMORIES

Professional memories lead teachers to adopt practices they found to be successful in the past and to reject practices that are unfamiliar or that they previously found to be unsuccessful. As shown in the research outcomes described above, teachers' worlds are context-bound, and so are their memories. Far-reaching changes in the context of teachers' work may conflict with their professional memories from previous contexts, thus posing difficulties in adapting practices to novel situations. Research on the impact of specific teaching situations on teachers' memories provides insights into this relationship, as shown in the following study of teachers' work-related memories.

The Impact of Teaching Situations on Teachers' Memory (Ben-Peretz 1995b) explored how different teaching situations affected memories of teaching events among forty-three retired teachers in Israel. The main source of data was interviews with these retired teachers, where they were asked to supply recollected events from their years of teaching practice. The recalled teaching situations were analyzed to determine if contextual and other differences emerged. The contextual differences analyzed included: (a) school level—whether a teacher taught in kindergartens or schools; (b) timing of the event—when the reported event occurred during the teacher's career; and (c) socioeconomic status (SES) level of the student population.

Analysis of the memorable teaching events elicited eight content categories: focus on students, interpersonal relations, rules and principles, teaching alternatives, teaching context, job difficulties, positive experiences, and negative experiences.

The data were first analyzed regarding school level. The results showed that, for each of the eight categories, significant differences emerged between retired kindergarten teachers' memories and retired schoolteachers' memories. For instance, due to the different context, kindergarten teachers showed more emphasis on relations with parents than schoolteachers. Kindergarten teachers are in daily intimate interactions with parents, whereas schoolteachers have fewer opportunities for such contacts. Another example was in expressing rules and principles, where kindergarten teachers focused mainly on rules concerning the students themselves but schoolteachers focused more on rules for interacting with peers (Ben-Peretz 1995b).

Regarding timing of the remembered events, findings revealed that approximately half of all recalled events occurred in these retired teachers' first years of practice. This outcome may suggest that the early years of teaching, full of pressures, excitement, tension, and novelty, are most memorable for retirees. However, for the present sample, a confounding variable makes it difficult to know if this was the main explanation for the timing of their memories. Coincidentally, the years in question were extremely significant, both historically and socially, in the life of the new State of Israel. Some of the main events that were recalled from these early years of the retired teachers' careers included the country's establishment and international recognition, the massive immigration of Holocaust survivors, and the influx of refugees from North African and Asian countries.

These political and demographic national changes created many difficulties for the educational system, which had to quickly accommodate a population that doubled in size and immigrants who lacked knowledge of Israeli culture and the Hebrew language. The teachers who participated in the reported research remembered these circumstances as having a profound impact on their professional experience, shaping the nature of their recollections of that period. Again, these findings reinforce the crucial importance of the sociopolitical context in determining teaching practices and experiences.

In addition to examining the influence of the general school context and historical period on the nature of teachers' memories, the research also focused on examining the impact of specific kinds of student populations on teachers' memories. Correlations were calculated between the eight content categories and the three SES levels depicting the students in the classroom: low SES classrooms, middle SES classrooms, and heterogeneous classrooms.

The results showed that one of the eight categories was clearly related to SES. The teaching context category, which refers to the participants' elaboration of details from remembered classroom situations, was highest for teachers of students from lower income families. For instance, one teacher recalled: "In the '80s a new school was built. . . . The population was very heterogeneous, new immigrants, old-timers, children from broken homes. I was the homeroom teacher of the fourth grade, with forty-four students" (Ben-Peretz 1995b, 40). Perhaps the greater discrepancies in socioeconomic background between the teachers and the low-SES students made these circumstances more memorable in the reported events.

Alongside the differences that emerged from the research on retired teachers' memories in various situations, some commonality of memory content did emerge. This finding may indicate teachers' collective memory (Halbwachs 1980), which constitutes their shared meanings as a community. Such communities of memories carry shared meaning from the past into the present and future. For example, the interpersonal relations category predominated in teachers' shared memories. Almost all of the teachers, across the board, seemed to attribute vast importance to personal interrelations in the context of their remembered work, whether with the young students or with their colleagues, the principals, or the parents. This emphasis by teachers on their remembered interpersonal relationships in the workplace differs from some previous descriptions of teachers. For instance, Lortie (1975) depicted teachers as more individualized than socialized and as interacting with one another only at the margin of their daily work due to the cellular nature of schools' organization and due to schools' time and space ecology.

In addition to the content of teachers' memories, memories also have an affective quality that impacts a memory's quality and availability (Conway 1990). However, Wagenaar's (1986) research indicates that both unpleasant and pleasant memories lose their "sting" over time. The retired teachers tended to mention more unpleasant than pleasant events. Both kinds involved a high level of emotion and personal significance. The more recent the events were, the more positive they tended to be.

Teachers who had more positive memories tended to have worked longer as teachers. Perhaps, with experience, teachers gain better expertise in handling difficulties and therefore teaching events were evaluated by the teachers as more successful and were remembered. On the other hand, it is important to note that while looking back at the overall teaching experience, the retired teachers viewed their professional career positively. They remembered the long hours and hard work as satisfying; they remembered individual students, difficult heterogeneous classes, and curriculum struggles. They felt a sense of satisfaction that they made a difference. As Connelly (in Ben-Peretz 1995b, xiii) states in his forward to the book, this finding is surprising and hopeful, especially after hearing the voices of overload and despair from teachers in recent years.

The study of teacher memories has a double implication for policy-making. First, it might offer policy makers a conceptual framework for viewing teachers' work as a major factor in policy-making. Several categories of teacher memories might be meaningful for designing and implementing policies. Among these categories, teaching context and interpersonal relations require special consideration. As shown in the literature discussed above, teaching context is a major influence on teachers' role perception. In addition, the memory study introduces another essential category for policy-making in education; namely, the importance that teachers assign to interpersonal relations in their professional lives. Second, the overall sense of professional achievement conveyed by the teachers in this study bears an optimistic message to policy makers, despite the difficulties of present-day education. The centrality of context considerations in teaching tends to disregard "time" as an essential factor in shaping this context.

THE TIME FACTOR IN EDUCATION

One of the most important factors in education, both in policy-making and its implementation, is time. When looking at the three major domains concerning policy-making in education—curriculum, teaching, and teacher education—the conception of time has important implications. The chapter entitled "Perspectives on Time in Education" (Ben-Peretz 1990b) examines the ways in which educational literature uses time as a construct. In that chapter, a distinction is made between several kinds of notions related to the concept of time: instructional time; curricular time; sociological time; and experienced-personal time.

Instructional time is the classroom time that teachers prescribe and in which students are engaged. Two major time-related concepts here yield insights into the teaching-learning process and into students' performance. One is "allocated time," referring to the time that the teachers assign to classroom activities, and the other is "engaged time," referring to the time when the students are actually involved in those activities. For example, a teacher may allocate a half hour to complete a science experiment in small groups or twenty minutes to write a brief essay in literature, but students may engage in the assignment for less than the time allocated or may clamor for more time because they feel the allotted time is insufficient. Individual differences generally emerge regarding the need for more or less allocation of time.

Understanding how instructional time is used in different contexts, for instance, in various subject-matter disciplines or with different student populations, is essential for improving the efficacy of curriculum and instruction. In relation to globalization processes and to the goal of teaching effectively within a global world, teachers should examine how much instructional time is dedicated to different sociocultural groups in the classroom and how much time is spent on teaching globally related issues, such as environmental studies and technology.

Another notion of time in education is *curricular time*, which includes the time allocations and the specifications for time use that curriculum developers prescribe. Curricular materials, such as student textbooks or teacher guides, tend to specify time allocations for certain topics, such as photosynthesis in biology or the French Revolution in history. Viewing time as a curricular resource, Fenstermacher (1985) claims that although teachers cannot be held accountable for the actual achievement of outcomes as mentioned in the curriculum, they should be accountable for the time spent on activities that may potentially lead to those desirable outcomes. From the perspectives of curriculum development as well as policy-making, timing can be seen as related to the question of what should be taught and when and how it should be sequenced over time (Anderson 1985). For instance, policy directives for teaching mathematics might include specific times and sequences for different tasks, thus reflecting priorities regarding the targeted skills.

A third notion of time in education is *sociological time*. Zerubavel (1981) associates patterns of social events and activities with different forms of temporal regularity, such as rigid sequential structures and fixed durations. It seems that the sequential order of events is usually well structured in the social life of the classroom. Examples of sequential structures for time are a student raising his or her hand before speaking in class or the teacher's presentation of new material before assigning a task on that material.

Likewise, the curriculum units presented to teachers tend to possess a sequential structure. Such sequencing is natural when based on the inherent characteristics of the subject matter, such as the sequence of teaching arithmetic. It can also symbolize the power structure of schools (Zerubavel 1981) and curriculum planners, for instance in cases where a school decides without considering student interests that active involvement in art education can only follow completion of science curriculum course work. Rigid curricular sequencing might limit the teacher's ability to develop and use curriculum potential and should be questioned while planning curriculum or policy.

Rigidness of time is found, as well, in the duration of teaching activities. Specific learning activities are usually associated with conventions that elicit certain expectations in the participants; for example, students expect teachers' presentations of historical events to last longer than group discussions on value issues. Changes in activities' duration within the curriculum might clash with the school's timetable and lead to difficulties in implementing the curriculum, especially if teachers introduce new content such as

environmental activities. Policy-making in response to globalization processes could modify the teacher's emphasis on certain content areas, thus
clashing with students' past experiences.

A fourth notion of time in education is that of *experienced-personal time*,
in which individuals perceive the temporal order. Insights into the personal
meanings of time are important for understanding both teaching and learning practices. Students from diverse cultural backgrounds may differ in their
perceptions of temporal order and sequence, creating misunderstandings in
classroom management, as shown in the study of immigrants' experiences
of classroom situations (see part I, chapter 1). Immigrant students in that
study seemed to misunderstand why teachers devoted classroom time to
play activities, which they did not perceive as teaching.

Knowledge about time and about issues concerning time in education
holds important implications for curriculum planning and implementation, calling for the participation of an expert on time when planning curriculum and instruction. For the same reasons, such a person should also
be included among policy makers. If the notion of time is to be considered
in school practice, teacher education programs should also introduce
special courses on the issue. For example, in such programs, teachers and
preservice teachers could participate in analyzing time as it appears in written curricula and in live or videotaped classroom settings. With regard to
the time factor in teaching, as with all of the other aspects discussed in this
chapter and in the previous chapter on curriculum, teaching issues cannot
be divorced from the consideration of relevant teacher education programs
and their implications for policy-making.

CONCLUDING COMMENTS

Teachers are generally perceived as the most important agents in education. The present chapter discusses relevant literature that deals with some
aspects of teachers' roles and their role perceptions. In keeping with the
heterogeneous nature of the student population and the diverse working
cultures in which teachers operate, this chapter places emphasis on the
impact of context on teachers' attitudes and classroom practices. Time and
its implications for teaching and policy-making are discussed here as well,
based on education literature. The issues of teaching context, including
time, teachers' role perceptions, and the professional issues that engage
them, are an intrinsic part of the holistic model for systemic policy-making
presented in this book. Teaching is conceived as depending, to a large
extent, on teacher education, which is the theme of chapter 7, closing the
triangle of curriculum, teaching, and teacher education domains.

7

Teacher Education and Policy-Making in Education

Valid and defensible educational responses to crucial global changes in demography, environment, economics, and present-day technology cannot occur without congruent programs of teacher education. Therefore, the impact of social and cultural situations on teacher education programs must be evaluated, and insights must be derived for policy-making.

SOCIAL AND CULTURAL INFLUENCES ON TEACHER EDUCATION

Teacher education programs play a central role in preparing qualified teachers. Within the complex platform of teacher education, global policies such as the spread of technology or the rise of multinational economic systems generate an inherent tension with the traditional cultural and social forces of local contexts.

To demonstrate the role that social and cultural elements play in teacher education, *Social and Cultural Influences on Teacher Education* (Ben-Peretz and Lotan, in press) presents the case of the United States, in which historically conditioned social and cultural factors have influenced teacher education. Perceptions of teachers have shifted from that of moral guides who instill values in their students to that of instrumental educators who prepare future workers for their occupations. As masses of immigrants arrived into the United States in the twentieth century, industrialization and urbanization processes were at their peak and schools became a central means for social mobility and economic opportunity. Consequently, teachers have become valued mostly for their academic knowledge and for the skills they could impart.

Academic knowledge and skills for competing in the globalized world cannot be the only major goals of education in this era of sociocultural diversity and inequality due to global demographic movements. Therefore, teachers might be expected to act as public intellectuals who combine theory and practice in the struggle for cultural justice and equity (Cochran-Smith 2000; Niemi 2000). These issues must be an inherent part of teacher education programs.

According to Hartley (2002), global issues may impact teacher education through three competing influences: that of economical globalization, that of the demand for a new knowledge base, and that stemming from cultural differences. Students are expected to become global citizens, meaning that they become creative and also critical thinkers who are able to contribute to the requirements of the global economy on the one hand, and thus to be part of the new information age, but also, on the other hand, to be actively engaged in promoting issues of equity and social justice.

An analysis of teacher education programs in different countries and cultures indicates several commonalities (Ben-Peretz and Lotan, in press). These include a growing demand for teachers to complete academic degrees; an extension of the number of years of preparation for teachers; an emphasis on professional competencies; and the formation of standards and requirements for gaining a teaching certificate. These cross-national commonalities reflect the effect of globalization, which emphasizes the teacher's role in preparing citizens for the future workforce and for living in the global world.

Teacher education programs are also influenced by local political, economical, and cultural contexts. Even as global ideas disseminate worldwide, they might be critiqued, reconstructed, and even resisted as part of the process of conceptualizing reforms in specific local contexts (Elliott 1999). Indeed, awareness is growing that in order to be effective, new ideas must become integrated with local beliefs and conditions. Hence, teachers and teacher educators now face the difficult task of establishing an all-inclusive education system based on global ideas while maintaining local cultures and traditions (Townsend and Bates 2007). The potential tensions between global and local educational orientations make this task even more challenging and complex. Moreover, perceptions of teaching and learning have changed considerably in the last decades (Lampert and Loewenberg-Ball 1998; Phillips 1995; Vygotsky 1978). Teacher education programs cannot ignore these changes.

INTEGRATING CHANGES IN TEACHING
WITH TEACHER EDUCATION PROGRAMS

The major message of the present book is that policy-making in education requires a holistic, systemic approach. Recent changes in the conceptions of teaching and learning, due to the impact of many processes including the four globalization dimensions described in part I of this book, require congruent changes not only in curricula but also at the heart of teacher education programs. The paper "When Teaching Changes, Can Teacher Education Be Far Behind?" (Ben-Peretz 2000) discusses the integration of such changes in teaching with congruent changes in teacher education.

For example, as discussed in Ben-Peretz (2000), the twenty-first century has brought about changes in perceptions of teaching that relate to its "transformative" effect. The transformative quality of teaching refers to the attempt to change students in some profound manner, and, through these changes, to render an effect on society at large. To a certain extent, all education can be viewed as transformative, because changing a person's knowledge base could have far-reaching consequences for that person's set of values and attitudes toward life as well as for his or her future social involvement. Although no one definition of teaching holds for all times and all places (Jackson 1986), the transformative view of teaching may be considered to be a common thread running through diverse approaches to teaching.

Yet, in order to successfully implement such transformations in students, they have to be preceded by relevant transformations in teacher education programs that are appropriate to future conditions of learning (Goodlad 1990). According to Goodlad, teacher education programs that do not include features of teaching that are closely related to the envisioned nature of future classroom situations are lacking in validity. An example is the growing involvement of information technology in schools, which requires similar instructional strategies in teacher education.

Another example of a change with repercussions for teacher education, as discussed in Ben-Peretz (2000), is a prominent theory that has inspired changes in the perception of the learning process. Vygotskian theory emphasizes socially shared cognitions as well as the role of the zone of proximal development, of language, and of mentors in the development of cognitive function (Vygotsky 1978). According to Vygotsky, learning occurs in social interaction situations and requires mentors to accompany the cognitive development of students. The term *zone of proximal development* signifies the necessity for teachers, who act as mentors, to be able to judge their students' understanding and how much support they need. These perceptions of learning have led to a shift toward "teaching for understanding," where teachers assist students in comprehending the underlying meanings of the material, discuss problems and ideas, and set challenging standards of learning (Lampert and Loewenberg-Ball 1998). Vygotsky's theory, and the ensuing changes in the perception of goals of teaching, should become central components of teacher education, not only as part of the conceptual knowledge base for teaching but also in the concrete practices of teacher education instructional strategies.

In addition to changes in the perception of teaching and learning processes, changes have occurred in the conception of the subject matter itself. Curricula in the twenty-first century include the introduction of new subject matter themes, such as environmental issues and peace education. It is unrealistic, and even counterproductive, to assume that new curricula in environmental education, or in crucial themes like education for peace, can be successfully implemented in schools without being part of teacher education programs.

Finally, another example of changes in teaching that require handling by teacher education programs relates to the growing role of technology in education. The massive amount of information provided instantly by the Internet, as well as interactive computer programs, are only part of the modern technology currently available at schools. Technology can contribute both to the learning process and to teachers' functions, provided that the teachers gain technological mastery and skills during teacher preparation programs.

Just as understanding school reform requires a complex view of the different factors it entails, so a reform in teacher education calls for a synergic approach (Ben-Peretz 1995a). The various and sometimes conflicting components of teacher education should be taken into account, trying to form connections between them. For instance, theoretical knowledge must be linked with practical work in the field while participating in a teaching practicum, and appropriate styles of teaching must coincide with forms of evaluation. If teaching relies, for instance, on problem-solving activities and on active use of knowledge in novel situations, then student assessments and evaluations must include similar cognitive demands.

Thus, the challenges posed for planners of teacher education programs today are many. A major dilemma of teacher education planning concerns how to deal with the pressures of global economic trends (with narrowing education budgets) without neglecting important humanistic ideas (Cochran-Smith 2000). Such a humanistic orientation espouses the development of autonomous teaching professionals who are able to respond to their students' needs as well as to strive for social justice. As preparation for market competition becomes a major goal of education, there is less and less room for teaching humanistic contents and values. Teachers are under more and more pressure to teach for standards and tests, thereby losing their professional autonomy and their ability to address their students' individual needs. In the face of global economic pressures, the task of teacher education nowadays might be almost impossible (Ben-Peretz 2001).

THE IMPOSSIBLE ROLE OF TEACHER EDUCATORS IN A CHANGING WORLD

The external pressures placed on teacher education at the present time due to global changes, in combination with the inherent demands of teacher education due to the professional needs of teachers and student teachers, have been previously discussed in "The Impossible Role of Teacher Educators in a Changing World" (Ben-Peretz 2001). That article argues that these external and internal pressures create a nearly impossible situation for teacher educators.

Such external pressures may include global changes that affect education, particularly the professionalization of teachers and teacher education and the emerging worldwide standards movement. At the same time, external experts in different content disciplines have issued an inherently incongruous recommendation for teachers to concentrate on teaching for understanding of subject matter and for reasoning in specific disciplines, rather than on rote learning and performance. Therefore, teacher educators frequently encounter difficulty in meeting these seemingly conflicting pedagogical obligations. For instance, ". . . according to Helsby (1999), a reorientation of schooling toward a functionalist view of economic development is inherently problematic because of its clash with liberal-humanist traditions committed to a belief in the non-instrumental value of education" (in Ben-Peretz 2001, 49).

Beyond these external pressures, teacher education is confronted, as well, with some inherent needs of student teachers and teachers. Light (1980), who analyzed the needs of medical students and physicians, argues:

> Technically, a profession's greatest need is for a better expertise in the form of knowledge and skills, but sociologically, a profession's greatest need is for control. Thus a major, implicit, goal of training in psychiatry and in other professions is to learn how to control the uncertainties of the situation at hand (282).

Like their preservice students, teacher educators frequently face uncertainty and seek to gain control when confronting the dynamic changes that they experience in our changing world, especially the impossibly competing requirements and expectations from teachers (Ben-Peretz 2001). Teacher education programs, both at the preservice and inservice levels, must take into account the powerful impact of teaching contexts and global influences and must plan means for responding to these effects and/or for furnishing resources for reflection and action. For example, as discussed in chapter 6, teacher educators must consider preservice teachers' deeply ingrained images and perceptions of themselves in their chosen role when attempting to foster these trainees' critical reflection skills (Ben-Peretz 2001). Furthermore, choices about effective teaching and learning vary drastically, depending on the preparatory program's primary aim (Labaree 2000). As Labaree asked: Does teacher education aim to foster democratic equality, thus preparing capable citizens? Or does teacher education aim to facilitate social efficiency, thus preparing industrious workers? Or does teacher education aim to enhance social mobility, thus preparing so-cial climbers who can efficiently compete for social "goods"? This chapter does not attempt here to solve these problems but rather to raise aware-ness of inherent difficulties of policy-making in education, which must consider the implications of any policy for seemingly impossible external and internal pressures on teacher education.

Issues influencing the design of new teacher education programs in light of changes in the perceptions of teaching and learning and the pressures of global changes are also introduced in Darling-Hammond's (2006) article, "Constructing 21st-Century Teacher Education." That article describes the main components needed for strong and effective teacher education.

First, a high level of coherence and integration should be achieved be-tween courses and clinical work. As mentioned above, it is crucial for teach-ers, especially novice ones, that theories of teaching such as the Vygostsky approach are experienced firsthand in their own teaching encounters, such as when the teacher encourages joint problem-solving discussions.

Second, proactive close relationships should develop between teacher education programs and schools to communicate models of good teach-ing that serve diverse learners. Collaboration between teacher education and schools means that teacher educators work in schools together with cooperating teachers and small groups of student teachers. Thus, theory and practice are joined in the service of student teachers and the improvement of schooling in professional development schools. Such interconnections between different elements of teacher education programs, as part of a synergic approach, resemble the holistic approach presented in the present book.

The realities of twenty-first-century schooling have increased the demands from teachers and hence brought forth a range of new teacher education goals. In today's society, education is viewed as increasingly important not only for the success of the individual but also for the nation as a whole, which is competing with other nations across the globe for economic suc-cess. As described above, global changes, such as the information highway, the rise of technology, and the need for students to function in a hetero-geneous worldwide community have made teaching a more complex task than ever before. Thus, teacher education programs must prepare teachers not only to master pedagogical content knowledge and understand the processes of effective teaching and learning but also to take into account the impact of language, culture, and community contexts on all these. In addi-tion, programs must prepare teachers to nurture every student despite his or her unique needs while effectively enabling a diverse group of students to learn complex material and practice high-order thinking.

Today's challenging realities of teaching require policy makers to build stronger models for teacher preparation. Importantly, as Darling-Hammond

(2006) recommended, teacher education programs must engage more closely with schools for mutual development toward transforming classroom settings. Policy makers must be informed about the intense, complex roles of teaching at the present time in order to consider these in their deliberations.

Teacher education may be viewed as an enterprise that has social responsibility. Teaching and teacher education influence, and are influenced by, social and political values, goals, and intentions. Hence, teacher education programs need to engage in public and political debates in order to have a meaningful voice in shaping teaching and society as a whole (Cochran-Smith 2000). This engagement might express itself in different ways. Public figures, such as writers or political scientists, might be invited to schools of education to meet with students and faculty to discuss societal issues. Student teachers might be expected to become engaged in public service activities beyond their practicum in schools. Faculty members of schools of education might voice their views on education issues in the media. A socially responsible view of teacher education that is open to public critique may have a profound impact on education policy.

The present book might help educational leaders formulate policies that account for global changes and incorporate innovative teacher education programs. The external and internal demands put upon teacher education programs, and teaching, should be regarded while planning these policies. Policy makers should take into account the bigger educational picture by considering what is occurring in teaching, in the world and society, and in teacher education. Such a synergic view of different elements could assist teacher educators in meeting their challenging responsibilities.

To produce extraordinary and well-prepared graduates, teacher education programs require the following common features: a clear and common vision of good teaching; well-defined standards of professional practice and performance that guide coursework and clinical work; and a strong core curriculum that is grounded in the understanding of child and adolescent development and learning, as well as in social and cultural contexts. Although a change in teacher education is only one component of high-quality teaching, it is a basic and essential one, and requires a voice in policy-making.

Both external global factors and local social and cultural factors can impact teaching and teacher education (Ben-Peretz 2001; Ben-Peretz and Lotan, in press). An education policy that aims to respond systemically to global changes and serve life in a global world, on the one hand, but remain relevant to different local contexts, on the other hand, should consider both global and local influences on teaching.

One example of the influence of local factors on education that must be considered by policy makers involves the social norms and regularities that may affect the uses of time in education. Examples of such norms and regularities concerning time are school hours and the length of the school year. New policies might introduce changes, such as shortening summer recess, which may contradict with local traditions of long breaks. Relevant policy would have to recognize some of the potential tensions between global and local influences on teaching and teacher education and account for them.

One way of dealing with these tensions could be greater flexibility of centrally constructed policy. Such a policy would heed the voice of local traditions (such as long summer breaks) while emphasizing global changes and trends (such as requirements for more time devoted, for instance, to environmental education). Perhaps professional educators should construct parts of education policy locally, considering the cultural and social factors that impact education.

The notion of curriculum potential presented above can be extended to "policy potential"; namely, the feasibility of adapting components of a central policy to local situations. Policy makers' specification of these components might be conducive to more effective local adaptations that nonetheless maintain common goals and requirements. Notions of local adaptations of policies in education should be incorporated in teacher education programs in order to prepare teachers for their role in implementing these policies.

IMPLEMENTATION OF NEW EDUCATION POLICY

While planning new educational policy, several issues concerning implementation must be weighed. Policy that seeks relevance and usefulness in practice has no choice but to include practical considerations. Planners of new education policy should therefore carefully consider the specific systems in which the policy is to be implemented. Is the policy expected to be applied within schools only, or does the policy address other possible target populations, like adults? What is the possible role of media in promoting the new policy?

A new education policy should examine the ideas it proposes in pragmatic terms, asking: Can they be implemented in today's practice or is a massive change in schools a prerequisite for their application? Will the proposed policy be applicable and effective in light of what is currently known about schooling and previously formed policies? In addition, planners of a new education policy should consider the role that long- and short-term goals are to play in the policy and ways in which teachers can be motivated to follow the principles of the new policy. Teachers tend to ignore individual student characteristics due to a need to simplify their complex role (McIntyre 2000). This situation can pose a problem for an education policy that accounts for the influence of demographic global changes on schools and calls for teachers to be able to deal with students' differences.

Planners of any education policy should consider various aspects of time usage. For example, what sequences and amounts of time should be devoted to what kinds of activities or curriculum materials so that they promote students' learning? Should certain determinations of time be prescribed at all? How can one incorporate new ideas into traditional uses of time? Viewing the importance of time regularities in education, changes might create uneasiness in teachers and students and could cause resistance to a new education policy.

Understanding and analyzing the ways in which teachers as curriculum implementers interact with the planned curriculum and form the enacted curriculum is crucial for an effective and relevant education policy. A new education policy should be conscious of the potential ways in which different stakeholders are likely to use it. A recurring problem is the limited ability of policy makers to predict the reactions of different stakeholders such as teachers, learners, or the public in general. Hence, policy should include an ongoing assessment process that involves drawing conclusions for improving the policy.

EDUCATION POLICY: ISSUES OF CENTRALITY

Policy-making that engages different societies and cultures faces the question of the extent of centralism. New policies in education are expected to deal with some globally shared issues. Shouldn't, then, some common guidelines and materials be derived from these policies? How can policy makers speak of common global changes and their implications for education without imposing them on local populations? The tensions between global and local concerns seem to be an inherent feature of policy-making. Perhaps a balance could be found between the local and global pressures, depending on the specific goals of the new policy. Some of these issues are addressed in part IV of this book, focusing on policy-making in education in the twenty-first century.

CONCLUDING COMMENTS

Viewing teacher education as necessary for valid responses to global changes, for instance, through curriculum endeavors, this chapter ties teacher education to changes in teaching and to social and cultural contexts. Both external global factors and local social and cultural factors are described as potentially influencing curricula and teaching and therefore as directly influencing the design of teacher education. If an education policy is to respond systemically to the needs imposed by the globalized world yet retain its relevance to different local contexts, then both global and local influences on teaching must be considered. The voice of local customs must be heard alongside attention to global changes and trends. As argued above, the task of teacher education is carried out in the context of competing external and internal pressures. Policy makers in education have to be aware of these difficulties and consider them in their deliberation.

One suggested means to navigate these sometimes conflicting pressures is for parts of the education policy to be locally constructed by professional educators while bearing in mind the effects of sociocultural contexts on education. This chapter recommends that the notion of curriculum potential can be generalized to "policy potential," indicating how feasibly components of a central policy can be adapted to local contexts.

Part III of this book looks anatomically at the process of policy-making from the point of view of my personal experiences and beyond. This next part presents concrete processes of policy-making and their relationships with issues of curriculum, teaching, and teacher education.

III

THE ANATOMY OF POLICY-MAKING IN EDUCATION: MY PERSONAL EXPERIENCES AND BEYOND

Part III Introduction

We now turn to concrete experiences of policy-making in education as they appear in changing societal contexts, influencing global trends. Any plan for new policy-making must include concrete examples in order to substantiate the conceptual framework that is presented. Hence, this part of the book first contains a brief narrative depicting some of my own involvements in policy-making in education, as chair of two policy committees. These two narratives, as well as a third case illustration on structural educational reform, all describe the context, the process, and the role of individuals as well as other forces in shaping policy-making. My experiences and those related to the substantive structural reform committee reveal some of the inherent difficulties and constraints of policy-making and provide necessary guidelines for the process.

Chairing policy committees is a complex and work-intensive position. Whenever problems arise that require possible policy changes, the Israeli Ministers of Education tend to appoint committees. Their work and recommendations are expected to guide policy-making and to provide the basis and support for policy makers' decisions. In this part of the book, I describe and analyze two cases in which I chaired such committees—one, on the reform of matriculation exams, and one on improving teacher education. Both cases are connected to global issues, as they reflect, on the one hand, the changing demographics due to immigration, and, on the other hand, the pressures of the global economy, which require appropriate responses in schools. The third case, on structural reform, clearly depicts the issue of global immigration as well as issues of societal integration and equity, which characterize many countries in the globalized world. Before my own experiences, I wish to present Walker's (1971) naturalistic model of curriculum development as a starting point for the cases below. A naturalistic model represents phenomena and relations that actually occur in educational processes. The model can refer to curriculum-making processes or to policy-making processes. Walker's model is a temporal one that postulates a beginning (the *platform* of developers' or policy makers' beliefs), a process (*deliberation* about different platforms), and an end (decisions comprising the curriculum's or the policy's *design*). This model does not attempt to be prescriptive but rather to provide insights into concrete instances of curriculum development. Walker's model offers some useful terms to describe and analyze processes of planning in education.

How is the naturalistic model *for curriculum development* carried out? According to Walker (1971), the process of curriculum development begins with the platform, the systems of beliefs and values that curriculum developers bring with them. This platform includes a vision of what is and what should be. The process continues by gathering data that support or challenge various platforms and are important for decisions that need to be made during the deliberation stage.

During the deliberation stage, different platforms are negotiated in order to reach a common ground and communal decisions. During this process, decisions are formulated, alternative choices are considered, and the most defensible ones are chosen.

Following this process, the curriculum design is formulated. The explicit design consists of decisions that were made after considering alternatives. The implicit design consists of unconscious choices that were made. The output is a set of decisions, not a list of objectives.

How is the naturalistic model *for policy-making* carried out? Similarly to the proposed process of curriculum development, policy-making also involves a platform that includes the participants' beliefs about education, about what is and what can be achieved. The scope, however, is larger than that of the platform of curriculum development because policy-making involves more factors to be considered. Conflicts might exist between differing beliefs and visions, especially if the policy committee includes different stakeholders and participants from diverse cultures. Here too, as in the process of curriculum development, a consensus should be achieved by a process of deliberation. The questions of what platforms policy-makers bring with them, how conflicting platforms are debated and joined, and how the deliberations take place are some of the issues that need to be considered in a viable model for policy-making.

I next present three cases of naturalistic policy-making in Israel that provide insights into this process. The implications of these cases for policy-making in response to global changes are noted.

8

The Case of Reform of the Israeli Matriculation Examinations

The committee on reform in the Israeli matriculation examinations was appointed by the Minister of Education in 1993 in order to examine a possible reform in the matriculation policy, a central facet in Israel's national secondary school assessment program. It is important to note that matriculation certificates are required for acceptance into Israeli universities and colleges (except for the Israeli Open University). Thus, matriculation examinations are high-stake exams, creating stress for students, teachers, and parents.

The committee, chaired by me, operated for one-and-a-half years. Members of the committee represented different stakeholders and interest groups concerning matriculation reform, such as teacher unions and university representatives. The committee gradually became a community with a shared purpose, a common language, collective experiences, and a growing sense of commitment. The process leading to this state is described and analyzed herewith.

REASONS FOR THE COMMITTEE'S FORMATION

The impetus for the committee's appointment was the current state of national educational assessment in Israel, raising the call for a change in the assessment policy. Based on Kingdon's (1984) model of opening a policy window, one might identify three key reasons for appointing the committee: an existing problem in the matriculation assessment program, the existence of an alternative, and a political climate in favor of change.

The first key reason for establishing the committee concerned the societal and pedagogical problems related to the exams. From a societal point of view, it was considered unacceptable that only about 40 percent of students finishing high schools in Israel were entitled to a matriculation certificate, although 71 percent of the cohort of students finished twelve school years. Moreover, significant gaps existed between different socioeconomic and ethnic groups concerning percentages of graduates granted matriculation certificates. From a pedagogical point of view, the amount of time devoted to preparation for the external examinations in the last years of high school denied students opportunities for meaningful and in-depth learning.

The second reason for establishing the committees was the existence of an alternative. Changes had transpired in the Israeli policy of school organization favoring decentralization, more school autonomy, and more school-based curriculum development. These changes created a basis for an alternative to the external examinations; namely, a reduction in the number of external examinations and a shift toward ongoing and varied internal, school-based assessments.

A third reason for the creation of the committee was the political climate, which was conductive to change at the time. The national labor government in office was interested in promoting equity and responding to the needs of diverse societal sectors through education. The then new Minister of Education strongly supported a reform in matriculation exams.

COMMITTEE MEMBERS

The committee included senior officials of the Ministry of Education, like the Director of the High School Department; the Chief Scientist; faculty members of several universities; chairpersons of teacher unions; school principals; as well as representatives of different school types including vocational, Arab, and Jewish religious schools. Altogether, there were sixteen members on the committee. Except for the Director of the Ministry of Education, all members attended the meetings regularly. The Minister of Education met once with the committee.

The whole committee met about every month for four hours over a period of a year-and-a-half, and no subcommittees were formed. Each meeting included a short break for refreshments and informal interactions. The chairperson generally set the agenda for each meeting, but committee members were involved in the process. It is important to note that representatives of various organizations and institutions were invited to voice their views. Among them were a member of the Knesset (parliament), a representative of the parent organizations, teachers of history and civics, and experts in measurement and assessment.

DILEMMAS AND CONFLICTS THAT AROSE
DURING THE COMMITTEE'S DELIBERATIONS

During deliberation, contradictory voices were heard and considered both inside and outside the committee, based on the different platforms of the participants. Contradictory cultural and political dynamics became apparent. For example, teacher unions and university representatives were opposed to any change in the existing matriculation policy. Both organizations exercised their great power in various ways, including the use of the media to present their point of view.

Teacher unions argued that a reduction in the number of external examinations would have several negative consequences such as harming teachers who teach subjects that do not require external exams, lessening students' motivation for studying these disciplines, and causing students with lower abilities to lose the opportunity to balance their grades in one subject area by their success in other subjects. The university representatives claimed that without external exams in a variety of subjects they would lack a valid, equal, and reliable basis for screening students who apply to enter institutions of higher education.

Members of the committee representing minorities, as well as religious and vocational schools, presented another source of conflict. They demanded consideration of their respective populations and needs. Thus, for example, Muslim and Jewish religious committee members wanted their respective subject areas to be included in the standards for mandatory external exams at a national level for students attending Muslim or Jewish religious schools, respectively.

Several essential dilemmas arose in the committee's deliberations. One dilemma emerged concerning cultural knowledge. Should all students share a common core of knowledge, or should the emphasis be placed on the cultures of diverse and heterogeneous student populations? Conflicting interests led committee members either to call for policy that met personal and societal needs by promoting excellence or to press for a commitment to equity and social integration.

As far as the dilemma that surfaced regarding the policy's scope, committee members revealed dichotomous inclinations: either to adapt a policy promoting school autonomy or to espouse a policy preserving the traditional Israeli centralized educational system.

One final dilemma that emerged was whether to demand teacher and school accountability to the Ministry concerning the achievement of centrally determined education goals or to encourage the conception of school goals that were not predetermined by the authorities and did not require feedback to Ministry officials.

Over time, members became involved in sincere attempts to coordinate their views with those of other members, to be receptive to others, and to relate to relevant knowledge and concerns of other members. Ongoing interactions with one another proved highly productive in generating conclusions acceptable to all committee members, with the exception of one.

INFLUENTIAL FACTORS DURING
THE POLICY-MAKING PROCESS

Several factors in the dynamics of the committee deliberations may be perceived as having a crucial influence on the final policy recommendations. One such factor is time. Though originally requested to submit their recommendations to the Minister of Education after four months, the committee members continued to deliberate for a year-and-a-half. This extension of time was deemed necessary for several reasons. The appointment of the committee created interest among educators as well as the general public, and many voices demanded to be heard. The committee received many letters and subsequently interviewed representatives from various interest groups, such as researchers, politicians, representatives of the union of school principals, and parents. Moreover, creating a community that collaborates on a joint task takes time. The move from overt antagonism of some participants to a more open-minded form of stating their views is a slow process.

Another factor that influenced the committee's deliberation process concerned the expectations that built up within the circle of participants, as well as outside it. Members of the committee were expected to reach operational conclusions. Although a number of officials in the Ministry of Education, as well as several professors of education, favored complete abolition of external exams, representatives of teacher unions and universities favored the status quo. As time passed, the Ministry of Education, educators, and the public reinforced the expectation for acceptable policy recommendations. Members of the committee felt a shared need to reach conclusions and were committed to doing so. Such commitment, and the effort to reach a consensus, led to a coordination of knowledge and experience as well as to compromise, which enabled a common final product.

RECOMMENDATIONS OF THE MATRICULATION COMMITTEE

The new assessment policy included in the final report, "Bagrut [Matriculation] 2000: The Report of the Committee to Examine Matriculation Examinations," submitted to the Minister of Education in 1994, represented ideological and practical compromises (Israel Ministry of Education, Culture, and Sport 1994). The report included details about the committee's formation, its mandate, and members. The history of matriculation exams in Israel and their goals was noted. The report presented details of the recommendations, including suggestions for their implementation. Appendices were attached, including empirical data (see Appendix). The number of subjects to be included in the matriculation certificate was not reduced, but part of the assessment process for three out of seven to nine compulsory subjects was to be transferred to the school. The number and nature of subject-matter disciplines was adapted to specific student populations and school systems (see Appendix).

An important aspect of the new policy was the modular format of exams. Three levels of studies were to be determined in each subject discipline: basic, standard, and advanced. Students who passed exam modules at one level would be able to progress to higher levels by passing an additional exam module on the appropriate curriculum components. The goal of this change was to enable students to gain growing confidence in their abilities, thus increasing the number of students eligible for a matriculation certificate. Once the new policy was approved by the Ministry of Education in 1995, and by all the relevant authorities, the problem of implementation arose.

POSTCOMMITTEE POLICY IMPLEMENTATION STRATEGIES

Policy implementation is part of a continuum that begins with the committee's first meeting and is a crucial stage in making the committee's work and recommendations meaningful. Implementation processes are handled by the Ministry of Education and are not part of the mandate of policy-making committees. In the matriculation reform case, the coordinator of the committee, who was previously director of the Department for Secondary Education in the Ministry, headed some of the implementation efforts.

The Ministry adopted two main complementary modes of reform implementation. One was the revolutionary mode of reform implementation, based on the authority and power of the Ministry in a centralized school system. Following the policy recommendations, the Ministry decided that no external exams would be held in three subject areas to be identified each year. In these subjects, final matriculation grades were to be school-based. The decision about the internally examined areas was scheduled to take place annually toward the end of the last year of high school.

The notion underlying this revolutionary mode of implementation was that students would need to maintain their attention to all of the disciplines studied, without knowing in advance on which subjects they would be tested. Yet, the exemption from three subjects was expected to reduce the inevitable pressures, stress, and workload on both students and teachers toward the overloaded end of the twelfth grade. At the same time, the remaining matriculation examinations in the majority of subjects would provide sufficient data on students' aptitudes and abilities to satisfy admissions experts in the institutions of higher learning.

The second mode of implementation was the evolutionary mode, a slow process of working with, and in, schools to search for ways to improve school-based assessment. New curriculum materials had to be simultaneously developed to match the new modular nature of testing. Ongoing consultations with university leaders and educators were needed to ensure the continuation of this process and to appease any opponents.

The evolutionary mode adapted was in the form of an intervention project in twenty-two high schools in Israel. These high schools represented various regions as well as ethnic and religious groups in different school systems, both academic and vocational. In each school, one to three subjects were chosen for school-based development and assessment. Teachers learned to use divergent modes of student assessment, and students became more involved in the learning process. New schools were expected to join the project in the future and serve as models for systemwide implementation of the matriculation reform policy.

As a strategy, combining the two implementation modes allowed for the synergy of diverse forces to interact and enhance the power of each.

THE DECLINE OF THE NEW MATRICULATION POLICY

After several years of implementation, the new matriculation policy was abandoned in 1999. General elections caused a change of government and the appointment of a new Minister of Education who decided to stop both modes of policy implementation. The only part of the policy to be kept was the modular format of the examinations, but all modules reverted to their formerly external derivation, outside the schools.

The short life of this new policy reflects the changing balance of power between individuals and societal forces (Ben-Peretz 2003). When the balance of power leaned toward a government that favored the reform, the reform implementation gathered momentum. Once power over implementing the reform was in the hands of a new Minister of Education who did not support the reform, the implementation of the new reform declined. The Minister also had the power to determine which parts of the reform policy he wished to implement, if at all.

Reforms in education seem to have a life cycle, from circumstances of birth to stages of decline (Ben-Peretz 2008). Yet, sometimes, a reform reappears. When a policy reform fails to be executed, a new reform is suggested, in a cyclic form of policy development (Ben-Peretz 2008). The present Minister of Education (in 2008) is again calling for a similar reform in matriculation exams.

PRINCIPLES OF SYSTEMIC-HOLISTIC POLICY-MAKING IN EDUCATION

An analysis of the policy-making process in the Israeli matriculation case provides some insights into broader principles of policy-making in education and illuminates the complexities of policy-making as well as its relation to educational practice.

- *Participants in the process.* The composition of the committee reflected the needs, concerns, and views of the different stakeholders and interest groups concerning matriculation reform. The members also included representatives of the various sectors that comprise Israeli society. Moreover, the public was involved as representatives of different interest groups, such as parents, who wrote to the committee and were interviewed by its members. These diverse participants constitute a kind of "rainbow coalition" (Nicholson 1989) mentioned above (chapter 6). By involving outside parties, the committee created a large interest in its work. Hence, the probability increased that its reform policy would be implemented by the relevant authorities and also fostered by the public.
- *Initiator/s of the policy-making process.* The reform initiative was raised by the Ministry of Education, which is the central decision-making power concerning education issues in Israel. This is indicative of the effect that political factors render on policy-making.
- *Reasons and causes for policy-making.* The reasons for the formation of the current policy-making were threefold, forming what is called a "policy window" (Kingdon 1984). First, dissatisfaction had emerged regarding the low percentage of students who were earning a matriculation certificate. Second, a change in the school organization policy was leaning toward decentralization. Third, the government supported educational change and addressed the issues of equity as well as the needs of diverse societal sectors. The reasons for policy-making included, altogether, dissatisfaction with the current state of assessment, relevant changes in pertinent educational policies, as well as a political desire for educational change. This situation illuminates the power that political parties have when it comes to initiating educational change. This same power is also manifested in implementing and maintaining the change, inasmuch as the Ministry of Education was responsible for implementing the committee's recommendations.

• *Factors that influence policy-making.* Several factors seem to have influenced the policy-making process. One factor was time: The extension of time for the committee's work created pressure to come up with acceptable recommendations. Another influential factor involved the expectations of the Ministry, the public, and the committee members themselves. The factors of time and expectations both contributed to the formation of a sense of commitment to create shared recommendations and to work collaboratively.

Though these factors may lead policy makers to overcome conflicts and work cooperatively, it must be noted that too much pressure placed on the time factor, and on expectations, might damage the deliberation process and lead to unacceptable results. Policy-making committees must be given sufficient time to form cooperative communities, to deliberate, and to know that they can rise up to meet expectations within a reasonable amount of time.

Another factor that influences the process of policy-making, and its product, is the relative power that different stakeholders have. For example, during the committee's deliberations, as discussed above, representatives of teacher unions and universities exercised great power in various ways in order to promote their stance. While forming a policy committee, the power of the different relevant stakeholders and interest groups, as well as the ways in which this power is exercised, should be considered.

• *The process.* The processes of policy-making begin with the context that creates the motives for forming a policy-making committee. It continues with the committee's deliberations, during which different and sometimes conflicting views, ideas, and concerns (platforms) are revealed and negotiated so as to form a committed and collaborative community with a shared language, vision, and experience. After the committee reaches a consensus, a product is formed that may constitute a compromise between the different platforms. Policy-making in the Israeli matriculation reform case thus reflects all three phases of Walker's (1971) naturalistic planning model: a beginning (the platforms), a process (deliberations), and an end (the design product). The committee completed its role with the submission of the report, the design product.

If the Ministry of Education accepts a committee's recommendations and decides to put them into practice, the implementation process starts, preferably combining complementary implementation modes that are appropriate to the educational contexts in which the reform is to operate. The process of changing the practice of teaching is an ongoing one, as the implementation of the committee's recommendations is constantly evaluated, reevaluated, and improved.

The matriculation reform report did include recommendations for the implementation process. It suggested several phases of gradual implementation over a five-year period, leading from the onset of this process to full implementation of the new matriculation policy. Aware of the need to systemically integrate the three domains of education, the report suggested the introduction of appropriate changes in preservice and inservice teacher education programs in order to prepare teachers for new strategies using school-based evaluation. The proposed changes in the structure of matriculation examinations required, as well, changes in the curriculum.

The product that the committee submitted to the Minister of Education was a report that included its decisions and recommendations. The product represented a compromise between the different representatives who participated in the committee. The product also reflected new trends in education in Israel that encouraged school autonomy, as well as the government's policy to promote equity and to care for the needs of the various sectors within Israeli society.

CONCLUDING COMMENTS

The case of reform in the Israeli matriculation examinations illustrates the naturalistic process of policy-making in education and its implementation. The existing problem in the national matriculation assessment program, combined with a political climate that supported change and the existence of alternatives for assessment, created momentum for the policy's formation and implementation. However, after a new government and Minister of Education were appointed, who did not support the new reform, the implementation process declined. Factors such as dissatisfaction with the current state of education, timing, politics, and collaboration among policy makers played a major role in the case of reform in matriculation examinations in Israel. In cases of policy-making, a volatile balance exists between the power of individuals and other societal forces. Whereas societal forces might promote changes in the nature of matriculation examinations in order to foster equity, individuals like Ministers of Education have the power to either support or prevent these changes. The same factors also influenced the case of the reform of teacher education in Israel, reported next in chapter 9.

9

The Case of Reform
of Teacher Education

This chapter presents another narrative depicting my own involvement in concrete policy-making in education. This second committee, to be described here, was founded by the Minister of Education in 2000 to examine the essence, structure, and process of teacher education in Israel in relation to the Israeli education system and its societal needs.

THE STRUCTURE OF THE NATIONAL
TEACHER EDUCATION SYSTEM

The Ministry of Education is accountable for supplying teachers to all sectors of education for all age groups nationwide. Educating the appropriate teaching force is an integral part of this responsibility. Teacher education in Israel is offered at three types of institutions: (1) Twenty-six colleges of education that train teachers from preschool to junior high school and award BEd degrees, accompanied by a teaching certificate; (2) departments of teacher education located at six universities, which train junior high and high school teachers, awarding a BA in an academic discipline and a teaching certificate; and (3) twenty-three ultrareligious Jewish orthodox seminars, where the training program lasts for two years and is nonacademic.

The nonacademic institutions are not authorized to give a BEd or a BA certificate and are not under the academic responsibility of the Council of Higher Education. All academic programs at Israeli universities are under the control and supervision of the Council of Higher Education, which is responsible for their approval. The Council of Planning and Budgeting is responsible for overall planning of academic institutions and for their budgets. In order to prevent political interventions in these processes, both the Council of Higher Education and the Council for Planning and Budgeting are autonomous by law though clearly connected to the Ministry of Education; the Minister of Education chairs the Council of Higher Education.

The Ministry of Education is responsible for teacher education in the colleges, according to the Compulsory Education Law (1949) and the State Education Law (1953) (Hacohen 1999). This responsibility includes budgeting, supervision, and awarding teaching certificates to college graduates. Academic responsibility for these colleges, as well as for departments of teacher education in universities, lies in the hands of the Council of Higher Education. There is a difference in budgeting responsibility. Universities are not funded directly by the Ministry of Education.

REASONS FOR COMMITTEE'S FORMATION

The impetus for this committee's appointment was the current state of teacher education in Israel at the time. There were several reasons for establishing this committee that I chaired. First and foremost, in the public eye and in the view of educators and thinkers across the board, serious criticism was being voiced against the education system. Both the processes and the outcomes of the current system of education for children and youth were being received with general dissatisfaction and disregard. Partially, this dissatisfaction was associated with the state of teacher education and the caliber of teachers in general.

Another reason was the increasing lack of candidates for teacher education, as manifested in low enrollment numbers in the various teacher-training programs all over the country. This drain in recruits to teacher education appears to be linked to a continuing decline in the status of the teaching profession as well as the proliferation of new alternative careers in other professions such as high tech, law, and medicine. Economic globalization also opened up new career options for prospective teaching candidates, especially women, who make up the majority of teachers. The status of teaching declined as easy access to knowledge bases over the Internet lessened the respect for teacher knowledge. Concurrently, due to migration, the teaching of heterogeneous classrooms became more and more difficult.

Last but not least, growing awareness about the unique challenges involved in educating citizens of the twenty-first century, in the face of globalization trends, called for a reexamination of the nature of teacher education and a refinement of its structures and processes. This awareness certainly contributed, too, to the initiation of the committee for developing a new policy of teacher education.

THE COMMITTEE'S MANDATE

In our initial meeting, we derived the questions addressed by the committee from the mandate given to it by the Ministry of Education. These questions addressed principles and practical questions regarding the essence and structure of teacher education in Israel. These questions were as follows:

- Should the special status enjoyed by colleges of education that prepare teachers be preserved as the only institutions preparing kindergarten and elementary teachers?
- How should the planning, budgeting, management, and supervision of teacher education institutions be organized?
- Who should have the authority to grant a license to institutions that educate teachers, which up to that time was only in the hands of the Ministry of Education?
- What criteria are appropriate for admitting students into teacher education programs? What incentives to candidates for entering teacher education programs are appropriate?
- What conditions should be required for granting teaching certificates?
- How can the needs of diverse societal groups such as ethnic or religious minorities be met in teacher education programs?
- How can the connection between teacher education institutions and the field be tightened?
- How can the implementation of pedagogical and organizational innovations in schools be assured?

COMMITTEE MEMBERS

There were approximately thirty members actively involved in the committee's deliberation. Members of the committee represented major stakeholders and included representatives of the academic institutions for teacher education in universities and colleges of education, as well as representatives from different sectors of education—general, religious, and Arab. Representatives of the Ministry of Education participated, too, such as the Director of Teacher Education and the Ministry's former legal consultant. In addition, representatives of teacher organizations; a representative of the students, the Deputy Chairperson of the students' association; and a representative of the Association of Colleges of Education were included in the committee.

The Minister of Education appointed the members. A number of officials from the Ministry of Education appeared before the committee during its deliberations and presented their views regarding various aspects related to teacher education in Israel. One of these officials was, for example, the Director of the Measurement and Evaluation Department in the Ministry of Education.

The participants were knowledgeable about different aspects of teacher education programs. A researcher and several administrative helpers assisted the committee. It is important to note that the Director of the Ministry of Education participated only twice in the deliberations, in the first and eleventh meetings, out of a total of fourteen meetings. Thus, the impact of ministerial preferences was kept to a minimum. On the other hand, the Ministry leadership did have the opportunity to influence the deliberations. The composition of the committee reflected the needs, aspirations, views, and interests of several groups of stakeholders: ministry officials, institutions, teacher educators, teacher unions, researchers, and student teachers.

The committee started to act in September 2000 and was revalidated by a new Minister of Education, who took office then. The committee began its assignment by approaching the public through advertisements in the newspapers, asking for feedback and suggestions regarding teacher education. Sixty messages were received, dealing with issues like strengthening the connection between colleges of education and public schools; recruiting high-quality human resources for teaching; nurturing student teachers and teachers both personally and professionally; and providing student teachers with the knowledge, tools, and skills needed for meaningful and successful educational practice. Alternative models for teacher education were suggested.

The committee also received position papers from researchers and from influential leaders in the education system. Position papers were submitted, for instance, by the Director of the Beit Berl Teacher Education College and by the Chairperson of the Education Committee of the Israeli Parliament (Knesset).

STRUCTURE OF MEETINGS

The committee conducted fourteen meetings, including two full days, eleven meetings that took several hours each, and a final meeting with the Minister of Education. Five subcommittees were formed to address the following issues: (a) general and special needs according to geographical and cultural environment; (b) criteria for licensing and supervision; (c) organizational and content structures; (d) the relation between teacher education institutions and schools; and (e) criteria for admitting student teachers and for awarding teacher certificates. Each subcommittee met several times and prepared reports that were discussed in the general meetings, leading to the final recommendations.

DILEMMAS AND CONFLICTS THAT AROSE DURING THE COMMITTEE'S DELIBERATIONS

The committee began with setting its agenda in the form of the questions presented above. It aimed at relating to three general aspects of teacher education: (1) its essence, that is, its purposes and goals; (2) organizational issues, such as the desired degree of autonomy for each college; and (3) the desired structure of teacher education. Throughout the deliberations, the chairperson repeatedly clarified that there were great expectations in the educational system and the public concerning the committee's task, and the committee's appropriate response was needed. The main expectation voiced by interest groups outside the committee was that the initiation of a change in teacher education would spark change in the education system as a whole. These expectations created a sense of responsibility, power, and strength among the participants, leading to a holistic consideration of large issues and frameworks. Still, discussions of different viewpoints and interests in the meetings, reflecting the different platforms of committee members, led to several conflicts among them.

An attempt was made to analyze commonalities among different opinions and suggestions so as to reach a common ground and present a unified document of recommendations. I expressed my hope "to reach a unified stand that will influence the Minister of Education and the Director of the Ministry" (meeting 5). I believe that "unified recommendations have a better chance to be implemented by the Minister and the education system. Hence, it is important to come to a compromise. If we cannot do that, the final document will include the different opinions" (meeting 12). Committee members agreed that consensus among them regarding the recommendations would strengthen them and would increase the likelihood that the recommendations would be accepted and implemented.

One prominent dilemma that began from the start of the deliberations related to the vehement conflicts that often appeared between the representatives of universities and the representatives of colleges. Both of these kinds of institutions were educating student teachers and competing for financial and human resources. Both types of institutions tried to convince the Ministry of Education that their mode of teacher education was most effective.

College representatives protested against what they viewed as overly high thresholds for admission into universities' teaching programs. University representatives, on the other hand, complained that the growing number of colleges already offering or currently designing teacher education programs raised concerns about preserving the quality of teacher education. An important dilemma concerned the possibility of merging several colleges into a few centers, creating large institutions and reducing the competition among colleges for talented recruits. Large centers would be more efficient financially as far as the staff and the physical campus are concerned. On the other hand, the needs of different demographic sections would not be appropriately addressed, and students who thought about registering for teacher education might be prevented from doing so due to the colleges' more centralized locations. Moreover, existing colleges were loath to give up their autonomy and specific programs.

Some of the committee members, as well as its chairperson, attempted to reach an understanding between the two sides by stating that no one ideal means of educating teachers exists and by reminding the parties of the high complexity of this profession and of the constantly changing conditions in the field. Several members suggested that the recommendations should not be biased toward either the universities or the colleges and that a balance should be reached between their interests.

The colleges prided themselves on their pedagogic competencies and on the value of the practicum they provide to their students. Departments of teacher education in the universities claimed that the preparation in subject matter knowledge provided by them is extremely important for becoming teachers. Each group of institutions argued for expanding the support granted them by the Ministry of Education and the government. Recognizing the value of each mode of teacher education was clearly important for reaching common ground. The Director of the Ministry of Education stated that "thinking differently is legitimate and desired. I suggest that the committee deliberates freely without fearing the consequences" (meeting 4).

Another inherent dilemma facing the committee related to the attempt to identify which problem characterizing teacher education should be considered as the major, key difficulty. Some members thought that the main problem originated in programs' entrance requirements. Others talked about budget issues or the teacher education process itself. Due to the complexities and problems of teacher education, it was necessary to address key issues and propose some valid solutions. In the final stage of the committee's work, a multifactor perspective was adopted.

Another dilemma centered on the scope of the committee's mandate. Members debated whether they should deal with specific issues, such as the pedagogy of teacher education programs. As chair, I reminded the committee that it was "expected to come up with general recommendations, and not with specific courses of action" (meeting 5). The committee agreed that recommendations were not expected to outline specific courses of action, like teaching strategies to be adopted by teacher education programs.

A further dilemma concerned the inclusion of different sectors of Israeli society into the deliberations. For example, debate arose as to whether the special case of the Jewish ultraorthodox sector of teacher education should be addressed in the committee discourse. The Jewish ultraorthodox sector in Israel prefers a secluded lifestyle, including separate schools and teacher education programs. Our general committee did not consider itself suitable to deal with the specific problems of this sector; therefore, the committee decided to exclude this sector from its deliberations. Members agreed that this decision would be stated in the committee's report and supported by the reasons for the sector's exclusion, along with a suggestion to establish a special committee to examine this specific sector.

Another conflict arose regarding the Arab and the state-religious sectors. Deliberations concerning these two sectors were regarded as clearly within the mandate of the committee; however, debate ensued as to whether the college teacher education programs for these two sectors should be kept separate or should be part of the secular teacher education institutions. (This debate concerned only preparation for teaching roles in preschool through junior high school, because teacher education for the senior high school level in the universities is not separate.)

The committee decided that the current status quo should be maintained, where college teacher education programs operate separately for the Arab and state-religious sectors in an attempt to permit the adjustment of the education system as a whole to the local needs of each of these minority sectors. It is important to note that despite the existence of several separate Arab teacher education colleges, many Arabs choose to study in general colleges.

These aforementioned dilemmas faced by this committee can clearly be generalized to other cases of policy-making, as well. For example, the latter dilemmas reflecting the multiethnic and multicultural reality of Israel have ramifications for policy-making in education in other heterogeneous countries, as well. Both the issue of general versus specific recommendations and the issue of inclusion/exclusion that arose in the context of this committee have general implications for policy-making bodies. How all-inclusive and far-reaching should, or could, their decisions be?

One way of resolving the dilemmas and conflicts was to search for the common basis beyond the different platforms. During deliberations, all arguments were considered respectfully and seriously. Over time, committee members were capable of compromise and of coordinating their views and platforms with those of others. For example, a member who had previously vocally opposed the university programs' autonomy outside ministerial authority was later able to state: "As a result of the things mentioned here, I was persuaded that there is no need to establish a single means of teacher education. . . . I do not think it possible that the university departments of teacher education can be governed by the Ministry of Education" (meeting 12).

INFLUENTIAL FACTORS
DURING THE POLICY-MAKING PROCESS

The committee wished to submit a final document of recommendations that would be embraced by the Ministry of Education and other stakeholders and would be implemented in practice. A variety of factors that were closely linked with teacher education had to be considered. First, budget considerations were imperative. Could the government provide the appropriate funding necessary to implement the committee's recommendations regarding teacher education?

Second, we contemplated whether the committee's recommendations would be congruent with the state of the field. Would the recommendations be applicable considering the current conditions, concerns, and resources characterizing the field of teacher education in Israel? For example, would the committee's recommendations diminish the autonomy of the universities?

Third, time pressures were a crucial factor. The Ministry was conveying a sense of urgency and was expecting practical solutions to pressing problems in teacher education. There was, as well, significant interest among educators and the general public concerning a possible reform of teacher education. Thus, tension arose between time limitations for the committee's deliberations, on the one hand, and the need for a sufficient period of time to allow the committee to solve conflicts and dilemmas through collaboration and coordination of views, on the other hand.

RECOMMENDATIONS OF THE
TEACHER EDUCATION COMMITTEE

The final twenty-six-page report that was submitted to the Minister of Education in December 2001 included a chronological description of the committee's formation, details about the committee's modus operandi, and the recommendations (Israel Ministry of Education, Culture, and Sport 2001). Appendices were attached, including empirical data and the reports of the subcommittees. The final report emphasized the need for transparency regarding the committee's work, allowing stakeholders and members of future committees to learn from the current one. The report's recommendations concerned two aspects of the teacher education process: (1) institutions and bodies that train teachers, and (2) the student teachers themselves. As mentioned above, one of the problems confronting teacher education in Israel concerns the lack of appropriate candidates for teaching. Therefore, several recommendations concerning recruitment and retention of student teachers were included in the report.

Recommendations Regarding Institutions and Bodies That Train Teachers

Regarding the training institutions, the committee made two recommendations, as follows. First, in special cases, academic institutions that currently were not yet educating teachers could be granted permission to award teacher certificates if (a) the Ministry of Education determined it was necessary, and (b) the institution met specific criteria outlined by the Ministry of Education and the Council of Planning and Budgeting, such as resource availability and program quality.

Second, in order to promote teacher education institutions in terms of their responsibilities, social status, and functioning, the committee suggested promoting the MEd degree studies in the colleges of teacher education as well as increasing the academic autonomy of colleges as a function of their academic advancement. As described above, one of the differences between universities and colleges of education in Israel pertains to the degrees they grant. Whereas universities grant BA, MA, and PhD degrees in the departmental disciplines (like literature or computer science) as well as certificates of teaching, colleges of education grant BEd and nowadays also MEd degrees and certificates of teaching but no academic degrees in disciplines. In order to equalize their academic status, colleges of education are interested in granting degrees in the disciplines, too. Therefore, the committee recommended that in special cases, the possibility for a teacher education college to grant a BS/BA in a discipline would be considered according to the needs of higher education and the educational system, depending upon local resource availability and the proposed programs' quality.

The representatives of the State Teachers Organization disagreed with these two recommendations. They recommended maintaining the current situation, which differentiated teacher education colleges from universities and other colleges. This disagreement was conveyed in the written report.

The committee further recommended that, in order to promote teacher education in Israel, the existing institutes be examined and mapped, while taking into account the requirements of different sectors, geographical locations, and specific resources. This mapping would lead to the merging of some local teacher education colleges into central colleges and to a wider allocation of government resources. The committee also recommended establishing a state database of the available human resources in teaching and teacher education.

Factors that might influence the training process and the teaching quality in the education system were also noted in the report. Among these factors were, for instance, the deteriorating status of the teaching profession and the insufficient quality of teaching in teacher education institutions. Teachers are perceived, first and foremost, in the widest sense, as educators. As such, they should possess intellectually wide horizons in many disciplines, expertise in their discipline of choice, as well as a solid knowledge base about the various cultural heritages interwoven into Israeli society and a commitment to democratic values. These qualities are of utmost importance in the Israeli education system, with its high level of heterogeneity within and among the different sectors and its abundance of new immigrants. Such qualities are particularly needed today worldwide, against the backdrop of dynamic global changes that demand young citizens' exposure to diverse subject matters and peoples in order to function optimally in a globalizing world. The committee outlined these needs and recommended both the inclusion of a liberal arts education and the nurturing of cultural heritage as part of recommended curricula for teacher education programs.

Recommendations Regarding the Student Teachers Themselves

Regarding student teachers, the committee recommended that in order to increase teachers' status and grant the teaching competencies necessary to address the growing complexity and demands of the educational system, admission requirements for teacher education programs should escalate. Excelling student teachers should be motivated academically, financially, and professionally. Such incentives could include granting students scholarships, reducing their number of years of study, or introducing a more flexible timetable to allow them better opportunities for engaging in teaching alongside their studies.

A STANDOFF IN DELIBERATIONS LEADING TO TWO PARALLEL RECOMMENDATIONS

On one issue—obtaining a teaching license—the committee was unable to reach a common stand. There was heated debate over the possibility of a state licensing examination. Such an exam was supported by some university representatives but was vehemently opposed by representatives of teacher organizations, students, and teacher education colleges, who were in favor of granting a teaching license based on the evaluation of an apprenticeship year. As a result of the committee's inability to reach one single conclusion about licensing, the report proposed two alternative recommendations. Option 1 was that receipt of a teaching license would require a successful evaluation following an apprenticeship year. Option 2 was that receipt of a teaching license would require a successful evaluation following an apprenticeship year, plus an appropriate external state exam.

POSTCOMMITTEE POLICY IMPLEMENTATION STRATEGIES

At the end of the committee's meetings, the Minister confirmed that she saw it as her "personal duty to apply the committee's conclusions with the help of the committee members" (meeting 15). Following submission of the report, the Ministry of Education did implement the committee's recommendations with regard to raising academic requirements for entry into teacher education programs and to undertaking attempts to merge colleges of education. However, again, as with the committee described in the previous chapter, political changes interfered with the implementation of much of the recommended reform in teacher education. Appointment of a new Minister of Education in 2006 meant that other issues were given priority over the reform of teacher education, and the remaining recommendations of the committee were disregarded.

PRINCIPLES OF SYSTEMIC-HOLISTIC
POLICY-MAKING IN EDUCATION

An analysis of the ways in which principles of policy-making were reflected in the committee's process of examining teacher education in Israel offers some general, broader insights regarding policy-making in education.

- *Participants in the process.* Members of the committee were representatives of the relevant stakeholders: heads of teacher education, members of education departments in universities and colleges, representatives of teacher and student organizations, and officials in the Ministry of Education. The composition of the committee reflected the needs, aspirations, views, and interests of several groups of stakeholders who sometimes held conflicting interests. Representatives of the different sectors in Israeli society were involved, as well. Though not represented directly in the committee, the media and the public were addressed at the beginning and asked for their opinions regarding teacher education in Israel. It is important to consider in advance who the potential stakeholders of a policy are so as to ensure their involvement in the process.

- *Initiator/s of the policy-making process.* The reform initiative was raised by the center of decision-making power in education in Israel, the Ministry of Education. This indicates how important support from political factors can be in expediting the policy-making process. The power of political bodies, and of the Ministry of Education in particular, is also evident in the committee members' and chairperson's call for consensus so that the committee's recommendations would be more likely to be accepted by the Ministry. Most policy-making committees in education can only make suggestions. Whether or not these are actually implemented in practice usually depends on political figures and their relative power.
- *Reasons and causes for policy-making.* The main reason for the committee's appointment was dissatisfaction with the current state of the Israeli educational system and the status of the teaching profession, both of which were partially attributed to problems in teacher education. Moreover, awareness was growing about the need for education of citizens of the twenty-first century, calling for a reexamination of teacher education as a whole, with an emphasis on its structure and resources. Generally, any impetus for policy-making changes seems to include both dissatisfaction with the current state of affairs and a look toward future changes and required adjustments. Policy-making in response to global changes, as well, needs to observe both the present and future in order to devise valid policies.
- *Factors that influence policy-making.* The issues of power, time, and the historical and cultural context are noticeable in the current deliberation process. Committee members including me urged the committee to try to reach a consensus, upholding that the power of the committee in handing out its recommendations lies in its unity. In addition, the power of political factors was evident, as the deliberation opened and ended with the Director of the Ministry of Education presenting the Ministry's stand.

  Another main factor that seems to influence policy-making is time. From the beginning, the committee was informed that it was expected to submit its conclusions within a year. During each meeting, the chairperson announced the time schedule for that particular meeting and for the committee's work in general. The time pressure was one of the reasons for forming subcommittees. A large committee that consists of many members and wishes to examine different aspects of a policy should consider forming subcommittees, which can set their own time schedules and present their suggestions before the general forum.

  A third factor that impacts the policy-making process is the historical and cultural context. From the outset, the committee members were presented with background concerning teacher education in Israel. The committee was concerned with the need to reexamine teacher education in light of the changes in education necessary to prepare individuals for life in the globalized twenty-first century. The political-cultural context played a major role in determining the committee's goals and in shaping the deliberations and product. One aspect of the cultural context refers to Israel's multicultural society. The committee members included representatives of the major sectors in Israel, Jewish and Arab, religious and secular, and so on. Lacking were representatives of immigrant sectors. Considering that mainly the mainstream sectors are under the supervision of the Ministry of Education, the committee mentioned the need to examine issues of teacher education in other sectors, such as the ultraorthodox community, by committees that would be formed especially for that purpose.

- *The process.* Analysis of the processes depicting the committee's work reveals that policy-making begins with agenda setting and continues with deliberations. Next comes the design phase, with the construction of conclusions and further deliberations as a draft of the product is created. More details on these phases are presented in part IV of this book.

The deliberation process was characterized by conflicts that arose between members of different representative groups. Unsurprisingly, conflict appears to be an unwavering factor in the process of policy-making. Each committee member follows his or her own ideology and philosophy concerning the issues at hand. In that sense, each member has his or her own platform, which represents their values and beliefs. The nature of issues and problems, the possible scope of policies, as well as the chances of realizing policy recommendations, must all be carefully considered in systemic policy-making.

To support and justify their stand, members of the present committee used statistics and research data in Israel and around the world as well as insights from their previous experience. The result was that several members changed their initial opinion, thus promoting coordination of platforms. Interestingly, representatives of teacher organizations consistently objected to the majority's opinion.

- *The nature of the product.* The product submitted by the committee to the Minister of Education comprised a set of recommendations that were theoretically grounded as well as operational. A policy-making product must coincide with the committee's mandate. In the teacher education case, recommendations were congruent with the committee's initial questions. Detailed reports of the committee's deliberation process is important, both as a means of raising the committee's validity and to serve future policy makers. Though reaching a common ground is important for policy makers and reflects a synergic approach, arguments diverging from the general opinion also need to be stated. This assures that the committee indeed represents different interests and voices.

CONCLUDING COMMENTS

The case of reform of teacher education in Israel elaborates the complex process of policy-making in one of the three central domains of education—teacher education. As in the case of reform in matriculation examinations, dissatisfaction with the current state of affairs, political power, and time were factors that influenced this policy-making process. It seems that implementation is the Achilles heel of policy-making. Any change in the political climate, central or local, might alter, displace, or reject policy decisions. Sometimes a revolutionary mode of implementation, as described in chapter 8, appears to have the power to sustain policies, but even then political shifts might terminate implementation. The following chapter, chapter 10, presents another concrete case of policy-making in Israel that highlights some of the impacts of ideological and political issues. In that case it is shown that synergy between the many different parties involved in policy-making is crucial for the policy's successful development and implementation.

10

School Structure Reform in Israeli Schools: An Example of Synergy in Education

This chapter presents another concrete case of policy-making in Israel that highlights some of the impacts of ideological and political issues, as well as the details of the process itself. I was not involved in this case personally but studied it after its completion (Ben-Peretz 1995a). As described above in the Introduction chapter, in the introduction to part II of this book, and in chapter 5, the Israeli school reform in the 1970s structurally metamorphosized the educational system's design. The prior system, comprising eight years of elementary school followed by four years of high school, was transformed at the time to a structure comprising six years of elementary, followed by three years of junior high, followed by three years of senior high schooling.

Initiatives in policy-making for education often result in reform ventures. The current description of the educational reform that transpired in Israel in the 1970s underscores some crucial issues in the planning and implementation of educational policies, with an emphasis on the merits of a synergic model for school reform. The *Babylon Online Dictionary* defines synergy as follows: combined action of two or more agents that produces a result stronger than their individual efforts; cooperation between two or more groups, combined action.

Such an approach can increase the likelihood that policy-makers can reach a more holistic view of the issues at hand, become better exposed to the multifaceted nature of any issue, and come to conclusions that are relevant to a greater variety of contexts. Synergy empowers the policy-making process by reflecting a consensus attained after engaging in open-minded deliberations. A synergic approach to policy-making also offers educators the chance to understand the complexity of an issue in depth and inspires them to find ways in which they can work in cooperation with others to try to make the best of a new suggested policy.

Some researchers and thinkers view educational reform from a conflict perspective, which perceives change as accompanied by ideological and social struggles and competition among groups (Ginsburg 1991). The present case exemplifies a different view of educational reform based on a synergic approach, which focuses on combining or correlating the actions of distinct groups to yield the desired consequences. Yet, the synergic approach does not mean that policy-making proceeds without conflicts and dilemmas. Both conflicts and dilemmas seem to be inherent to the process of policy-making.

The notion of synergy explains the success or failure of policy ventures, especially during implementation. The collaboration and coordination of the various factors involved serves to create great momentum toward successful policy-making, a sum power that is greater than the accumulation of individual forces. A similar approach was described in chapters 8 and 9, where members of policy-making committees worked cooperatively to reach a shared view and to bridge conflicts that arose during deliberations. Thus, for example, representatives of different sectors in Israeli society, teachers and teacher educators, college and university representatives, and the like were able to share their platforms, debate on their different views, and reach a common ground in most issues.

REASONS FOR THE COMMITTEE'S FORMATION

During the late 1960s and early 1970s, comprehensive junior high schools for grades 7 to 9 were first formed in Israel, only two decades after the establishment of the state. At that stage, the country was still attempting to form a unified nation of numerous immigrants from various countries, cultures, and backgrounds. The impetus for this structural educational reform stemmed from a perceived lack of academic rigor during the last two years of elementary school, a high percentage of failure and dropout at the postelementary stage, a correlation between failure and geocultural origin, and the homogeneity and segregation of elementary schools (Inbar 1981).

GOALS OF THE NEW EDUCATIONAL POLICY

The structural reform aimed to improve students' achievements and increase social integration. The first goal was to be achieved through "instrumental integration" (Yogev 1989), establishing intermediate schools as a means of promoting the academic achievements of students of Asian-African origin in Israel. The second goal was to be achieved through "symbolic integration" (Yogev 1989), forming intermediate schools as a national-ideological goal in itself, as a symbol of equity. The reform's implementation served both functions.

INFLUENTIAL FACTORS DURING
POLICY-MAKING AND IMPLEMENTATION

In 1987, the reform had been implemented in 70 percent of municipalities, affecting about 55 percent of students in the relevant age group. Evaluation research from 1987 indicated that integration in the intermediate schools had shown a positive and consistent, though weak, effect on the achievements of students from low socioeconomic backgrounds. Furthermore, by 1988, the gap had narrowed between the different geocultural groups regarding rates of success in obtaining 11 to 12 years of schooling (Dar and Resh 1988).

Although the Israeli school reform seemed to be yielding fairly positive results, its process of implementation was arrested by the 1980s and the 1990s. In 1977, right-wing parties were able to form the first non-Labor national government since the establishment of the State of Israel. The new government channeled funds to neighborhood renewal programs rather than continuing to support the education reform that had been started by former Labor governments (Ben-Peretz 1997).

In line with a synergic approach, several factors appear to have interacted simultaneously and created the perceived positive results of this structural reform. Many parties were involved in the process of implementing the intermediate school reform. First, central and local authorities like the Ministry of Education, the Israeli parliament (Knesset), and the local municipal authorities played a role. Second, various stakeholders collaborated in the implementation, including teacher organizations, principals, teachers, parents, and so forth. Third, parties external to the school system were involved, such as political organizations, the Supreme Court, scientists, teacher education institutions, and so on.

The first to formulate and outline the new policy were governmental authorities and the Knesset. The Labor Party, which was the majority in control of the parliament at the time, supported the reform. At the beginning of the policy's formation, the national teacher unions violently opposed it. The elementary teachers' union feared that the structural change reducing the elementary school grades from 8 to 6 would damage the status of elementary teachers and even diminish their numbers.

Changes began when the Ministry of Education appointed a public committee to implement the new policy. Municipal authorities were delegated responsibility for implementing the reform, and they enacted the committee's recommendations all over the country, changing physical plants of existing school buildings, designing new separate school buildings for junior highs, publicizing the changes in the media, and preparing students and teachers for the new structure. In addition, under the guidance of the Ministry of Education, new curricula were developed for junior high schools in all subjects.

Once the reform was accepted in most municipalities, though not in all, the national teacher union endorsed it, recognizing its contribution to teachers' professionalization and higher salaries. Scholars had also adopted the desegregation principle, and academic research helped sustain the new policy (Klein and Eshel 1980; Yogev 1989). Yogev argued that Israeli researchers had "adopted the school desegregation principle as a major yardstick for evaluating the contribution of the school system to equal opportunity" (78). The parents' response to the reform was mixed, but many parents kept a low profile concerning the reform, mainly because its administrative, economic, and pedagogic decisions did not clash with societal and political ideas of the time.

As a result of this structural reform, changes and improvements in teacher education programs were recommended in order to meet the novel professionalization demands for those teachers entering positions in the new junior high schools. However, such changes were mainly executed in teacher education institutions controlled by the Ministry of Education. Specifically, BEd programs were introduced at the time into teacher education institutions to increase the professionalization of teachers. Changes in curricula and teacher education that accompanied the new structural policy in Israel are evidence for the need to integrate these domains into the process of policy-making in education. As seen in this case of structural reform, synergy is best achieved through collaboration and coordination of different bodies in the process of policy-making and implementation as well as through the integration of different domains in education.

Despite this seeming consensus about the reform, some groups strongly contested the change, and its implementation was hampered by tough opposition, mainly by parents who feared the impact of student integration on academic achievement. The slowing down of the policy's implementation in the 1980s was partly due to the aforementioned political reverse in Israel in 1977, as the new right-wing government was interested in major economic and social improvement in low socioeconomic areas and did not believe in the power of the new, integrated junior high schools to contribute significantly to this goal. Major projects of social renewal in disadvantaged localities were initiated at this time.

BROADER IMPLICATIONS FOR POLICY-MAKING,
PARTICULARLY IN RESPONSE TO GLOBAL CHANGES

In sum, synergy can be considered an appropriate framework to account for the process of school reform. This chapter proposes that synergy between different relevant parties is actually crucial for the development and success of an educational policy.

In all policy-making, as seen throughout this part of the book, potential problems can arise when deep, inherent conflicts emerge between different parties. In such cases, attempts should be made to reach some common ground. As different parties interact during the policy's development stages, emerging conflicts can serve as a constructive impetus for uncovering key aspects of the reform that need thorough consideration. Uncovering potential difficulties is necessary for establishing some common ground and for finding solutions to emerging problems.

As mentioned in chapters 8 and 9, time and timing play a crucial role in this process. Timing is connected to the political issues of opening a policy window. As time passes, practical problems present themselves, and those solved successfully in one locality serve as models for other localities. Although central and local authorities often appear to clash over issues of autonomy and control, these parties seem to complement each other's efforts in implementing the new policy. The structural school reform in Israel was centrally decreed, triggering some negotiations about local autonomy on the path to obtaining municipalities' agreement to implement this policy. Collaboration between center and periphery turned out to be very fruitful.

Many of the parties mentioned in this chapter should also be considered as exceedingly relevant to the process of policy-making in light of globalization changes. Such parties include: central and local authorities, stakeholders, and parties external to the school system. For example, an educational policy that accounts for the impact of global changes on education must gain the support of governments, Ministries of Education, and local authorities, and must also consider various ways in which such support can be achieved. Responding to global changes might require, as well, international cooperation and the support of international bodies like UNESCO, OECD, and others.

Finally, this chapter posits changes in curriculum, teaching, and teacher education, as complementary and necessary for a policy's implementation. This calls for an educational policy that would holistically consider the three educational domains and include representatives of each one in the policy-making bodies.

CONCLUDING COMMENTS

This final chapter of part III presents an example of synergy in a policy-making process by describing the structural reform that irrevocably altered the Israeli school system during the 1970s. Synergy between the many different parties involved in policy-making is crucial for the policy's successful development and implementation. The next and final part of the book suggests that such synergy among the three domains of education is vital, as well, for the success of policy-making. Careful collaboration and coordination among the various agents involved in policy-making are features of the holistic approach to policy-making presented in part IV.

There is an important distinction between policy-making that is concerned mainly with present problems, like the three cases described in part III, and policy-making in education that aims to respond to current and future global changes. The latter requires a consideration of future developments in the environment, demographics, economy, and technology of the country and also the world as a whole. Conflicts and dilemmas are natural phenomena in these endeavors, but policy makers must strive for synergic effects, pursuing the collaboration and coordination of the diverse groups and domains involved in the process.

Part III presented detailed descriptions of the complex interactions that characterize policy-making in education. Highlighting the cardinal impact of policies on this process, and the instability of implementation efforts, raises a crucial warning. Policy-making in response to global changes must not fail, nor should the implementation of these policies be at the mercy of political upheavals.

IV

Policy-Making in Education in the Twenty-first Century

Part IV Introduction

Let me start this section with an allegory. There is a saying: "If the horse you're riding dies, get off!" But the steed of education, however much it falters or disappoints, cannot be summarily abandoned. What are the alternatives? Sarason (1996, 315) mentions a few:

- Buy a stronger whip.
- Try a new bit or bridle.
- Switch riders.
- Move the horse to a new location.
- Ride the horse for longer periods of time.
- Say things like, "This is the way we've always ridden this horse."
- Appoint a committee to study the horse.
- Arrange to visit other sites where they ride dead horses efficiently.
- Increase the standards for riding dead horses.
- Create a test measuring our riding ability.
- Compare how we ride now with how we rode 10 or 20 years ago.
- Complain about the state of horses these days.
- Come up with new styles of riding.
- Blame the horse's parents. The problem is often in the breeding.
- Tighten the cinch.

This allegory offers a compelling way of explaining why school reform is such a difficult task and how one might find ways of circumventing the issues by suggesting bizarre causes and impossible solutions. In spite of the difficulties facing policy makers who pursue appropriate reform, educators must continue to maintain optimism about the possibilities for successfully achieving reform policies.

In part III, several cases of policy-making in education in Israel were presented and analyzed. These cases represent examples of a "natural model" of policy-making, which does not necessarily reflect theoretical models, in the same way that Walker's (1971) naturalistic model of curriculum development does not adhere to normative models. Here, in part IV of the book, the "naturalistic" models are discussed in relation with other models of policy-making and with relevant conceptual frameworks. Following this discussion, I propose an integrative holistic framework in a synergic manner for policy-making in education in response to globalization changes.

This fourth part of the book begins with some general comments on the nature of policy-making in education—the process, its components, and the various factors and agents that influence this process. Different modes of policy-making are analyzed.

11

Modes of Policy-Making in Education

> Education systems change slowly and require a complex process of planning and implementation. The challenges facing education systems currently require new knowledge about policy priorities and effective interventions for making the desired changes. The degree to which this knowledge can be created and shared collectively may make the difference in how this knowledge translates into new educational practices (Rosekrans 2006, 13).

As Rosekrans asserted, collaboration is key to successful policy implementation, whether at local, national, or international levels. Yet, not everyone is convinced that collaborative policy-making in education is carried out in fruitful ways. Levin (1998, 137–38) claims that:

> What is happening in education internationally is not best described as a process of mutual learning. Countries seem to be doing similar things, but on closer examination they are not as similar as it first appeared (Halpin and Troyna 1995). Particular bits are taken out of a country's approach and adopted elsewhere as if context did not matter.

Squarely facing the issue of context, Levin suggests the term *policy epidemic* as appropriate for present-day changes in policies of education. According to Levin, applying such epidemiological ideas to education policy changes can yield some important insights. Epidemiologically, both the environment and the nature of individuals are critical determinants in the occurrence of disease. Similarly, the take-up of any education policy idea depends greatly not only on the political and social environment at a given moment but also on "individuals—such as ministers, key officials or other influentials . . . [who] may play an important role in a particular setting"

(Levin 1998, 139). The approach for policy-making proposed further on in this book views the "context" for policy-making, which must be taken into account by all parties in the process, as conceived systemically. Such a conception includes both environmental characteristics like the sociocultural, political, and economic features, and also the personal characteristics of the relevant agents and stakeholders involved in the educational issues at hand.

The epidemiological metaphor for policy adaptation suggests some additional interesting questions in cases of opposition to reform initiatives, such as "Why do some communities seem to be resistant to certain policies? Is this an issue of immunization?" An important lesson to be learned from Levin is the need to consider local circumstances and conditions in any attempt to make policies that respond to global changes.

Such local considerations can be found in an interesting and valuable report of El Salvadoran policy-making (Rosekrans 2006), which has implications for the model proposed in the upcoming chapters of this book.

THE CASE OF EL SALVADOR

From 2002, the United States Agency for International Development in El Salvador worked for three years together with the El Salvadoran Ministry of Education and other central stakeholders "to support a series of participatory assessments and studies that led to changes in education policy" (Rosekrans 2006, 1). The new educational policy concentrated on "expanding educational opportunities to the poorest sectors and ensuring that all primary school children become numerate and literate" (7).

Rosekrans presents several lessons to be learned from the dynamics of this process, highlighting in particular the timing, circumstances, and political context as crucial factors shaping policy. She claims that it is vital to understand the internal dynamics of the decision-making process and to identify both allies and opponents, against the political backdrop of the time period at hand. Interestingly, the conclusions that Rosekrans draws from the El Salvador case of policy-making are conceptually similar to Schwab's (1964) approach to curriculum development, accentuating the need for varied tools and instruments to foster joint deliberations and the coordination of intentions and views:

> Tools are valuable for focusing discussions and for collectively constructing knowledge and building consensus. Tools could involve surveys, facilitated discussions, problem trees, frameworks, or any other means of leading a discussion toward the understanding of complex situations. For example, instruments that lay out policy options and gauge potential effectiveness and

viability can help to focus discussion and generate consensus (Rosenkrans 2006, 2).

Moreover, Rosekrans underscores that the people involved in policy-making must dedicate some thought to reflecting on their existing assumptions. These deeply held assumptions are referred to as "platforms" by Walker (1971) in his naturalistic model of curriculum development. Rosekrans argues that "it is helpful to have divergent perspectives represented to provoke the validity of deeply-held assumptions" (2006, 2). Coordinating divergent perspectives might lead to a committed, integrative "rainbow coalition" (Nicholson 1989). Divergent perspectives may be linked to ideologies (for instance, integration versus segregation), and they also stem from different knowledge bodies, such as cognitive psychology or sociology of migration, or from different interest groups or stakeholders, such as government and teacher unions.

The following examples of policy-making show the intricate relationships among the different components of the policy-making process, leading to a discussion of commonalities and differences among modes of policy-making in education. Such an analysis allows policy makers to learn from different contexts and to emulate what could be considered appropriate and effective for their own context.

POLICY-MAKING IN LATIN AMERICA

I start with the presentation of an analysis of policy-making in education from Latin America in the 1990s (Grindle 2004). Grindle's analysis provides important insights into the relationship between policy-making, politics, and economy as well as insights into the issues of power and timing. Integrating research findings on policy-making in education from several countries provides the basis for unfolding some generalizations. One of the reasons for presenting Grindle's analysis is its similarity with the analysis of the Israeli cases discussed further on, in spite of cultural and historical differences between Latin America and Israel.

Phases of Policy-Making

Grindle's analysis traces the phases comprising the process of reform in Latin American countries (e.g., Brazil, Bolivia, Chile, Argentina), beginning with the agenda-setting phase, progressing through the design, adaptation, and implementation phases, and finally reaching the sustainability phase. "Each of these phases can be understood as an arena in which political and bureaucratic interactions take place and affect what happens in subsequent arenas" (Grindle 2004, 16).

Parties Involved in Policy-Making

Grindle mentions a wide array of stakeholders involved in the process of policy-making in its various phases. Some of these stakeholders may be individuals; others are organizations. Among these are political leaders and parties, executive bureaucracies, municipalities, courts, and interest groups such as teacher unions, parents, media, and so forth. Thus, in Latin American countries, the reform process is characterized by conflicts and struggles among different stakeholders, with teacher unions usually in opposition to the planned reform. Several factors play a crucial role in the process: the relative power of participants, be they presidents, ministers, or unions; the strategies adapted by the diverse players; the timing of the initiative, and the initiative's unfolding through the various phases of the process; as well as the historical and cultural context.

Factors Influencing Policy-Making

According to Grindle's analysis, several factors may be hypothesized as associated with the initiation and sponsorship of reform initiatives at the agenda-setting phase; namely, economic and political conditions as well as the reform design teams and conflict.

Economic conditions may promote policy reform, whether economic crises or growth. In such cases, the reform protagonists are usually motivated by a larger set of goals, such as efforts to shift to a market economy or to alleviate poverty. Sometimes international organizations play a role in reform initiatives through financing, as can be seen in World Bank loans. As discussed in part I of this book, globalization has a far-reaching impact on worldwide economy. The Grindle study shows the relationships between economic considerations and policy-making in education.

Another aspect of reform agendas concerns the impact of political forces and conditions. One of the most interesting findings of Grindle's (2004) analysis is the following:

> Rarely, however, do major policy reforms get on national political agendas simply because a good case can be made for their importance, because evidence accumulates about the deficiencies of the existing system, or because new ideas stimulate interest in alternative ways of structuring and managing public responsibilities. Instead, almost always, problems become priorities on public agendas through political action (p. 28). . . . For reform to get on national political agendas for action, it must have political salience as an issue and influential voices to promote it (44).

In Grindle's study of political timelines as related to reform, initiatives during national elections did not seem to have an impact on election outcomes. The "honeymoon" period immediately after elections in Latin American countries was not characterized by an introduction of reforms in education. However, this finding pertains to reform policy in education and may be irrelevant for policy-making in other areas such as housing or environmental issues.

Successful reforms may be related to a favorable relationship between the executive and the legislative branches of the government. Yet, even this hypothesis does not explain reforms in several countries in Latin America, where some executives found a way to promote reform initiatives even without legislative majorities. Public opinion, though, may be an important factor in sponsoring reform. It is worth noting that "while public opinion signaled that education was important, it did not consistently guide politicians to select quality-enhancing reforms as a reasonable response to citizen interest in the sector" (Grindle 2004, 50).

Sometimes national meetings, conferences, and congresses stimulate reform initiatives, though these generally do not put forward concrete ideas about necessary changes. Most of the public involvement in reform in Latin America expressed itself in the mobilization of elite groups, such as universities. Very few grassroots groups such as parent associations or local citizen organizations were found to actively organize themselves to demand reform. Mobilized interest groups seemed to have been more influential in getting issues onto the political agenda. Grindle claims that "there is some evidence to indicate that politically influential groups were concerned about education prior to the reformist initiatives" (Grindle 2004, 51).

Altogether, Grindle (55) identified some generalizations about agenda-setting dynamics, stating that:

> An analysis of twelve cases found that presidents and other high-level officials largely controlled when and how education reform was raised in political circles. They also played a major role in determining why the issue of education was important to pursue. Thus, specific education reform initiatives could largely be understood as elite projects that emerged from centers of decision-making power.

Grindle's analysis highlighted two other major factors of influence in education policy change: the reform design teams and conflict. The reform design teams are considered major, strategically important actors in the reform process:

> How they designed the policies defined who would be the winners and losers in reform and how much they would win or lose. Moreover, their credibility, their interactions with more traditional bureaucrats in public sector ministries, their role as gatekeepers for participation in reform discussions, and their efforts to enlist domestic and international supporters were critical to subsequent conflicts and reform destinies (Grindle 2004, 21).

The analysis of Latin American countries underscored that conflict also seems to be a consistent factor in policy-making. One crucial conflict phenomenon concerns the role of teacher unions, who, as mentioned above, almost consistently oppose reform. In the case studies conducted by Grindle, the unions were central actors resisting the new initiatives. Governments used various approaches to deal with this situation, trying to create alliances that would help them manage the opposition. Sometimes governments negotiated with the opponents over the content of the reforms.

The Grindle analysis of policy-making efforts is compared below to other cases of policy-making. I start with the Israeli school structure reform because it highlights some inherent similarities between policy-making in Latin America and Israel.

POLICY-MAKING IN ISRAEL

This is a report on the conclusions of a study on the reform policy in Israel in the 1970s (Ben-Peretz 1995a). In the section following this one, the Latin American and Israeli cases are compared.

As shown in Ben-Peretz (1995a) and described earlier in this book (see the Introduction chapter as well as the introduction to part II and chapters 5 and 10), the Israeli junior high school structural reform of the 1970s had two main goals: (1) to improve scholastic achievements, and (2) to increase social integration. These two goals are especially meaningful for policy-making in response to global changes that require appropriate knowledge, on the one hand, and pose crucial societal problems as manifested by multicultural populations, on the other hand.

Phases of Policy-Making

Analysis of Israel's policy-making process from that period yielded the following model comprising several phases:

- *Agenda-setting phase.* To open a "policy window" (Kingdon 1984) that sets the agenda for policy reform, a combination of three "streams" is necessary. First, a "problem stream" must exist, referring to a set of conditions conceived as necessitating remedial actions. Second, an "alternative stream" must also be available, referring to a set of proposals for actions. Third, a "political stream" must be present, referring to public mood, pressure groups, and ideological views. As shown above in chapter 10, all these conditions existed in the Israeli case.
- *Design phase.* Once a policy window is opened, a policy committee is assigned and begins its deliberations. Several factors impact the delib-

eration process: the composition of the committee, time frames, joint expectations, pooling of knowledge and coordination, and formation of a community with a common language and goals.

- *New policy output.* The committee's deliberations lead to a new policy through consensus and compromise.
- *Implementation phase.* Once it is designed, the policy must be implemented. Two complementary modes of policy implementations may be adopted. In the "revolutionary implementation mode," significant top-down change transpires as a direct consequence of a central force (namely, the Ministry of Education), which pushes for and then regulates such a change. The other mode of policy implementation is the "evolutionary implementation mode," which is characterized by a slow, bottom-up process of working with schools and searching for gradual ways to improve the current state of local education in light of interpretations and transformations of the new policy. In the Israeli case, each school out of twenty-two schools that participated in this process worked independently, yet was assisted by a central regulatory body. The latter mode includes ongoing consultation with universities, teachers, and parents. This process of interpretation and transformation of new policies is similar to the process of using "curriculum potential" (Ben-Peretz 1990a) and the phases of curriculum transformation (Goodlad et al 1979) as discussed in chapter 5. As suggested in Ben-Peretz (1995a), the optimal means to promoting an ongoing process of change is to achieve synergy between these two modes of policy implementation.

Parties Involved in Policy-Making

As described in chapter 10, the following were some of the parties involved in the planning and implementation of this policy:

- Central and local authorities such as the Ministry of Education, Knesset (parliament), and local municipal authorities.
- Stakeholders such as teacher organizations, principals, teachers, and parents.
- Parties external to the school system such as the Supreme Court, scientists, political parties, and institutions of teacher education. As in the analysis by Grindle (2004), political forces are one of the factors seen as impacting reform initiatives in Israel (Ben-Peretz 1995a).

The analysis of two other Israeli cases of educational reform presented in chapters 8 and 9 underscores basic similarities to the junior high school structural reform, regarding the agenda-setting features involved, the influential parties, and the phases of the process. In part III above, "The Anatomy of Policy-Making in Education: My Personal Experiences and Beyond," this process was highlighted from the standpoint of my personal experiences with matriculation policies and with teacher education policies. Altogether, the analyses of these three cases allow for a comparison of the "Israeli case" with that of the "Latin American case," as seen next.

COMMONALITIES BETWEEN POLICY-MAKING IN THE LATIN AMERICAN AND ISRAELI CASES

Several commonalities characterize the processes of reforming education policy in Latin America and Israel, regarding the phases, involved parties, and factors influencing the process:

Phases of Policy-Making

In both the Latin American and Israeli cases, the policy-making process begins with an initiation phase, continues through deliberations among policy makers, and ends with a final product. During the deliberation phase in both cases, as conflicts and dilemmas arise, the changing balance between powerful individuals and vocal groups in the community may lead to the implementation or rejection of the policy.

Parties Involved in Policy-Making

In both cases, the list of stakeholders involved in the process is quite similar, with teacher unions trying to prevent the proposed reform.

Factors Influencing Policy-Making

In both cases, the power relations, and especially the power of governmental figures such as presidents or Ministers of Education, determine the fate of new policies. In both the Israeli and Latin American contexts, ideology, too, plays a crucial role in making and implementing policies in education. Miller and Fredericks (2000, 2) emphasize the role of ideologies in the formation of social policy: "The formulation of social policy often supports ideologically-based belief systems that selectively utilize 'scientific' findings." According to these scholars, the impact of social science on policy-making is negligible, and the findings of social science research are largely irrelevant to the process.

In sum, in all three main parameters of policy-making presented here—phases of policy-making, parties involved, and factors influencing this process—many important similarities emerged between the two cases. As a result of these common patterns and contents for the main parameters, they should all be incorporated in any systemic model for policy-making in education. Indeed, as can be seen in chapter 13, these parameters play an important role in the holistic model proposed in this book, which focuses specifically on responses to globalization.

CASES OF POLICY-MAKING IN EDUCATION IN OTHER COUNTRIES

The following are some concrete examples of policy-making in response to global challenges, one concerning recent initiatives in the teaching of science and technology in England and New Zealand (Jordan and Yeomans 2003) and one relating to literacy agendas (Lo Bianco 2004). Literacy constitutes a crucial issue in the global economy and is strongly linked, as well, to immigration in that it creates multilanguage populations. Both cases emphasize the role of ideologies.

Science and Technology Policies in England and New Zealand

The first case compares new approaches to science and technology education in England with those adopted in New Zealand, as responses to the challenges posed by the forces of globalization and the growing importance of the "knowledge economy." Jordan and Yeomans (2003) compare and contrast two science and technology education initiatives, one concerning technology colleges in England and one concerning science and technology teacher fellowship schemes in New Zealand, as policy responses to the knowledge economy and globalization. However, these authors argue that:

> . . . despite the different character, organization and practices employed by the technology colleges and the fellowship schemes, both initiatives are still embedded within a policy regime that looks backwards rather than forwards (67).

As seen here, both countries' initiatives were described as being concerned only with observing the present and past conditions in science and technology education and with raising awareness and appreciation of what scientists and technologists do, while rigidly maintaining the status quo. By contrast, a forward-looking policy regime should adopt a critical perspective on the effects of science and technology in a globalizing world, placing a premium upon flexibility and innovation in order to facilitate coping with unpredictable, upcoming global phenomena (Jordan and Yeomans 2003).

In their comparative analysis, Jordan and Yeomans situate England and New Zealand along a continuum of possible educational responses to globalization from a variety of ideological perspectives as defined by Wells et al. (1998): neoliberal, liberal-progressive, realist, and post-Marxist. Neoliberals "call for an end to the burdensome and out-dated 'welfare state,'" which includes state-run educational systems. In contrast, "liberal-progressive modernizers call upon policy-makers to invest more heavily in the state-run educational system and to create higher, more challenging goals and standards" (50). Realists claim that national educational systems have grown more like each other in certain ways. Rather than a full-scale globalization of education, the realists suggest "a partial internationalization of educational systems and not the end of national education per se" (53). Finally, the post-Marxists argue that public and private investment should be geared toward hiring labor so that investments in educational programs result in significant net gains in employment and help students from the poorest countries and families.

Jordan and Yeomans (2003) situate the policy responses in England and New Zealand as approximating the liberal-progressive approach, which approaches globalization as inevitable and sees a role for the state to protect citizens against its worst effects. The education system is viewed as "having a crucial role in producing the 'knowledge workers' required to compete in the global economy and which helps to deliver economic growth" (Jordan and Yeomans 2003, 66). These authors suggest that:

> . . . the frequent use of concepts associated with globalization in contemporary policy discourses actually masks an on-going neo-liberal agenda that has systematically attempted to harness teachers', parents', and students' capacities to the dictates of the market through notions of accountability, standards, efficiency and performance. The absence of any debate over the curriculum at present only serves to further this agenda (Jordan and Yeomans 2003, 80).

Jordan and Yeomans's conclusions about the dangers of a liberal-progressive approach underlying policy in western, English-speaking countries without considering the curriculum at whole support one of the main arguments of the present book; namely, that curricular considerations are essential for any policy-making enterprise that endeavors to respond effectively to global changes. Accountability and standards might be important issues in any attempt to prepare workers for a global economy, but without deep consideration of curricular issues, education is transformed into a servant of economy. Curricular considerations concern content as well as values. They deal not only with what is taught but also whom you teach and how to teach in ways that promote equity. The British and New Zealand cases of policy-making relate to changes in economy and technology but ignore demographic and environmental issues.

Literacy Agendas in English-speaking Countries

The second case of policy-making processes relates to power, policy, and professional knowledge in the literacy agendas of English-speaking countries (Lo Bianco 2004). In literacy, as in science, a strong connection seems to exist between a global economy and policy-making. For example, in the 1990s, the Organization for Economic Cooperation and Development (OECD), the international organization that endorses principles of representative democracy and free-market economy, adopted the notions that the:

> . . . developed national economies had lost competitiveness in international markets, and that this loss was partly due to literacy deficiencies. . . . Governments have been motivated to institute a kind of contract, in which the elevated importance of literacy within public policy is conditioned by restrictions on the professional judgment and autonomy of teachers (Lo Bianco 2004, 1).

Lo Bianco introduces two important basic concepts with an impact on policy-making in education: human capital and social capital. By human capital, Lo Bianco means the OECD definition: "The knowledge that individuals acquire during their life and use to produce goods and services or ideas in market and non-market circumstances" (1). Social capital, on the other hand, deals with the trust, goodwill, and networks of human collectives, rather than with isolated individuals. Policies inspired by principles and understandings of social capital would emphasize community-based settings and the networks of relations and social cohesion in which learning takes place (Coleman 1988; Putman 1995).

These concepts are meaningful for understanding the social background for policy-making in education. Policy-making that is motivated by the notion of human capital required in the era of economic globalization tends to focus on the preparation of individuals for serving the economy. On the other hand, concern for social capital might lead to an emphasis on the needs of communities, both locally and internationally. These tendencies might conflict with one another, and the outcomes of such a conflict are determined by the power relations among policy makers.

Policy-making itself is seen by Lo Bianco, as by Grindle and Ben-Peretz, as strongly related to power relations: "Policy does not emerge unproblematically from the demonstration of need. All new information is absorbed within power configurations that combine prevailing ideologies, existing knowledge and the various interests of those involved" (Lo Bianco 2004, 2). Indeed, issues of power relations must be incorporated into any model of policy-making, especially that responding to global changes, where powerful agents might be in conflict. Approaches to the policy-making process have changed over time:

> In the 1950s, under the direction of its main American proponent Harold Lasswell, emerging practices of "rational" policy making were codified and given the name "policy science." Drawing on incremental thinking and pragmatism, the policy sciences aimed to bring knowledge to ruling in a systematic way (Lo Bianco 2004, 4).

Nowadays, the view is that a different approach is needed. The "scientific" models of policy-making do not seem to be capable of dealing with the real-life complexities of problems requiring policy responses. Instead, it is contended, herewith, that an ecological approach, considering the interaction of manifold factors, is more appropriate.

Indeed, a prominent American policy analyst, Lindblom (1990) has stated he could identify very few success stories in three decades of public policy analyses of cases based on pragmatic and rational policy science. For Lindblom, it is preferable to use the "ordinary knowledge" of those affected or most closely involved with the consequences of policy choices in framing decisions rather than the specialized, arcane register of technical-bureaucratic operations (Lo Bianco 2004, 4). "Ordinary knowledge" of those involved with policy choices is represented, for example, by the knowledge teachers possess concerning classrooms. Likewise, Lo Bianco (5) discusses these points in his analysis of policy-making concerning literacy, where he advocates the inclusion of multiple stakeholders and representatives:

> The claim that "multiple methods" of inquiry should be adopted in a policy appropriate to these times would insist that the voices of literacy students, teachers, parents, academic researchers would be included within policies that would seek to fashion a kind of life-long learning and multiple settings approach for provision of funded literacy teaching.

As shown throughout part III of this book regarding the preferred participants in policy-making committees, Lo Bianco (2004, 6) emphasized the crucial need for multiple voices in order to achieve valid policy-making:

> It is precisely the absence of the diverse, contrasting and contesting voices, the cultural diversity of contemporary society, that are missing from policy conversations. There is little real evidence that the kinds of complexity of perspectives that might be expected to inject into policy considerations about complex and multiple literacies get to shape present policy.

This approach, espousing the need for a "rainbow coalition" (Nicholson 1989) that encompasses manifold voices in the process of policy-making, is adopted in the present book.

CONCLUDING COMMENTS

Policy-making in education is a demanding process, often characterized by conflicts and complex dynamics. The policy-making model to be presented in the final chapter of this book (chapter 13) attempts to meet this challenging task. In an effort to understand the process of policy-making in education and identify factors that influence it, the present chapter first illustrated policy-making through analyses of cases in Latin America, Israel, England, New Zealand, and other countries. These analyses, as well as the Israeli cases and the literature discussed previously in part III, together provide the basis for presenting an overview of the factors and stakeholders that influence education policy in chapter 12.

12

Factors and Stakeholders That Influence Education Policy

In order to suggest a model of policy-making in response to globalization changes in their various dimensions, the parties and the factors that influence education policy must be clarified. Swanson and Barlage (2006) asked leading education policy experts to identify and rate highly influential agents ("influentials") in four categories: studies, organizations, people, and information sources.

As to be expected, Swanson and Barlage found strong interconnections among these four categories of influential agents. Institutions, for instance, may be mentioned in several categories beyond the organizations category, as a home for renowned experts (information sources) or as sponsors of leading studies.

INFLUENTIAL STUDIES

Studies, like research documents, or surveys conducted by government agencies render an influence on education policy that comprises an interesting category, because studies attempt to narrow the oft-noted gap between research and policy-making. Swanson and Barlage identified as influential studies broad bodies of collections of works rather than individual reports or publications. This is not surprising because policy-making requires sound evidence for making decisions, and large-scale studies that rely on several sources seem to provide such an evidential basis for policies. Examples of general reports are the National Assessment of Educational Progress or the TIMSS (Trends in International Mathematics and Science Study), both from 2003.

It is important to note that the most influential studies, as rated by Swanson and Barlage's leading education policy experts, were evaluation studies. Measurements and evaluations (such as empirical studies documenting poor scholastic achievements or gaps between minority and majority students) rather than educational principles (such as the right to integration or equality) are perceived today as the major stimulus for policy-making in education. One of the main reasons for experts' reliance on evaluation studies may be the view of schooling as preparing the workforce for a global economy. For example, Beyer and Liston (1996) argue that the curriculum functions as an instrument for strengthening particular initiatives to strengthen competencies in areas that are useful for the economy and for avoiding a critical perspective on society.

INFLUENTIAL ORGANIZATIONS

First and foremost, influential organizations are government entities that are responsible for policy-making in education. Second, it is interesting to note that philanthropic organizations are also perceived as playing an important role in shaping education policies. In the United States, one example would be the Bill and Melinda Gates Foundation. In Israel there are several philanthropic organizations, like the Rashi Foundation, which spends large amounts of money on schooling and influences education policies, especially at local levels, by introducing their own curricula into schools, including assessment practices. Third, in many places, such as Western or Latin American countries, teacher unions are organizations that render a crucial influence on the processes of making and implementing policies in education.

INFLUENTIAL PEOPLE

As distinct from studies and organizations, influential people comprise a category that demands special attention. People conduct studies, and organizations are run by people. These individuals are decisive in shaping studies and polices of organizations. For example, when people in positions of power or influence switch jobs, as when a newly elected political leader appoints a new Minister of Education, the outgoing Minister's policies of education may undergo significant transformations (as seen in the cases described in chapters 8 and 9).

Therefore, in the United States, high on Swanson and Barlage's 2006 list of people who have shaped policies in education were President George Bush (for example, for his No Child Left Behind Act of 2002) and Senator

Edward Kennedy (the senior Democrat on the Health, Education, Labor and Pensions Committee in the U.S. Senate). In Israel, people like Yuli Tamir, the Minister of Education since 2006, and Abraham Burg, who chaired the Committee for Education and Culture in the Israeli Knesset (Parliament) in the 1990s, are considered examples of persons with influence over policies of education. In Britain, examples of major politicians who influenced policy-making in education are Labor Prime Minister James Callaghan (who, for example, called in 1976 for a core curriculum of basic knowledge), and Prime Minister Tony Blair, who emphasized the need to respond to the needs of each student.

Sometimes a full-time academic gains an influential role in education policy. One example is Stanford professor Linda Darling-Hammond, who served between 1994 and 2001 as the executive director of the National Commission on Teaching and America's Future.

INFLUENTIAL INFORMATION SOURCES

In the globalized information society, influential information sources should be regarded with particular care. Such sources may include traditional print publications as well as new media outlets. The media may make or break any attempt at changing policies in education. For instance, detailed newspaper reports on the low achievements of students in international evaluation exams may stimulate large-scale efforts by the Ministry of Education to introduce new policies aiming at improving grades and at raising standards.

The Swanson and Barlage (2006) study holds many implications for planning an optimal model of policy-making in response to global changes. Their study of highly influential agents:

- Demonstrates the complex web of interactions at play between the various influential agents, specified within four main categories: studies, organizations, people, and information sources.
- Provides policy makers with a tentative list of representatives who should be invited to participate in policy-making groups, including representatives from each of the four categories.
- Enables policy makers to make valid decisions about priorities of influences according to their specific contexts. For example, when a very strong and militant teachers' union rejects a new policy, policy makers have to make decisions about ways to overcome this opposition or to change the intended policy. At the time of this writing, a new policy in Israel entitled *Ofek Hadash* (New Horizon) that attempts to change the working conditions of teachers in the elementary and junior high schools is being highly contested by one major teachers' union.

- Suggests criteria for evaluating and judging the process of policy-making and its potential for success. Analyzing the process of policy-making in any of these four categories might uncover lacunas, such as disregard of influential information sources.

SUMMING UP: COMMONALITIES BETWEEN CASES OF POLICY-MAKING IN EDUCATION

The previous chapter (11) presented cases of policy-making in education in different countries and cultures, such as Latin America, Israel, Britain, and New Zealand. These cases might be viewed as naturalistic models of policy-making. The policy-making cases described above seem to have several features in common that appear to be crucial for every process of policy-making. These shared features concern the influentials (as described above in this chapter), the phases and processes of policy-making and implementation, and temporal and financial factors.

The Influentials

The policy-making initiative usually originates from, or is at least highly supported by, the Ministry of Education or other high-level political figures. The power of political factors in the process is also notable at the end of the process, as it is the Ministry that ultimately decides whether and how to implement the policy. Moreover, local governmental municipalities may be the ones responsible for implementing a policy in the local contexts, and therefore they, too, have great power in the policy-making process. Teachers' organizations do not usually have the power to initiate a reform, yet they can and often do block it by resisting change.

Scholars and researchers in academic fields seem to have less influence in affecting policy-making than do political or social organizations, though evaluative studies do render an impact on the initiation of policies. Powerful social organizations of influence might include a dynamic organization of citizens for saving the environment or a prestigious charity working for the benefit of underprivileged populations. The media are perceived as another powerful factor in the policy-making process, inasmuch as they can serve as an information source linking the public and the policy-making body.

Phases and Processes of Policy-making

Commonalities in phases and processes are also observable in all the cases described above. At the start, several prerequisite conditions must be present in order to initiate any policy-making process. These include dissatisfaction with the current state of education, a government that supports a change, and the existence of potential alternative modes of education.

Across the board for all the aforementioned cases, the deliberation phase is the time when different members of the policy-making body express their views and when attempts are made to reach a consensus of opinion. During this phase, the recommendations and/or conclusions of the policy committee are formed. Conflicts often arise during deliberations, but these might even be useful for developing the process. Nevertheless, a consensus regarding the final product must be reached.

Once a final document is created, the Ministry of Education, educators, municipalities, and the educational community are responsible for implementing the new policy and developing it further. The product could include both conceptual and practical recommendations and conclusions. During the implementation process, continuous evaluations need to be carried out in order to assess the policy's success and relevance to educational concerns.

TEMPORAL AND FINANCIAL FACTORS

All of the cases show that factors of time and finances are important both for framing the policy-making process and for forming and implementing recommendations. There might be pressure exerted by the expectations voiced by the public, by educators, and by the Ministry of Education for a time frame within which an appropriate policy should be formed. Financial matters are also crucial for the implementation of policy recommendations. Decisions about the allocation of funds may be in the hands of presidents or Ministers of Education but may depend as well on Ministers of Finance, the government, or parliament.

The insights gained from the analysis of cases of policy-making (in part III and in this and the prior chapter) all call for the application of a systemic, ecological model for policy-making that responds holistically to global changes and incorporates the three major domains in education (curriculum, teachers, and teacher education). Next I describe such a model, and in the following chapter, I propose several guiding principles for it.

AN ECOLOGICAL APPROACH

Weaver-Hightower (2008) argues that "policy creation is an extremely complex, often contradictory process that defies the commonly held image of singular purpose and open, effective planning" (153). The policy-making model proposed in the upcoming chapter of this book meets the challenge of addressing this extreme complexity by adopting an ecological approach, as suggested by Weaver-Hightower.

This approach has been used before. For instance, Sarason (1996) viewed schools as ecological entities, and Banathy (1996) conducted a system inquiry and its applications for education, among others. Barab and Roth (2006) also used an ecological framework for talking about curriculum. Weaver-Hightower expends the notion of "policy ecology" and defines it as follows:

> A policy ecology consists of the policy itself along with all of the texts, histories, people, places, groups, traditions, economic and political conditions, institutions, and relationships that affect it or that it affects. Every contextual factor and person contributing to or influenced by a policy in any capacity, both before and after its creation and implementation, is part of a complex ecology (155).

This extremely complicated definition is proposed by Weaver-Hightower as a framework for policy analysis. In the service of the framework's usability, Weaver-Hightower suggests four categories for analyzing policy-making: (a) actors, people who perform society's various roles (e.g., doctors, teachers, students, politicians); (b) relationships among the actors, manifested in competition, cooperation, predation, or symbiosis; (c) environments and structures such as schools and other social structures and institutions; and (d) processes that impact the relationships among actors and between them and the environment, such as entropy, when an ecology breaks down and becomes disordered. The model proposed herewith is intended for policy-making and not policy analysis and attempts to reduce the complexities to a manageable framework.

CONCLUDING COMMENTS

It is crucial to understand the factors that influence policy-making in education and the ways in which they operate in a policy-making model. This chapter presents four categories of influential factors: studies, organizations, people, and information sources (Swanson and Barlage 2006). All these factors are joined in complex ways and determine to a large extent the process of policy-making in education and its implementation, through their participation in policy deliberations. Understanding the nature of influential factors, as well as the intricacies of the phases and processes of policy-making, and, finally, its temporal and financial factors, provides the basis for the holistic model proposed in chapter 13.

13

A Holistic Framework for Policy-Making in Education in Response to Global Changes

In this chapter, in culmination of the main parts of this book, I now discuss the major issues at play in policy-making and propose a systemic model based on an integration of the four globalization dimensions (part I), the three educational domains (part II), the detailed reports of case illustrations for educational reform committees (part III), and the analysis of policy-making processes, which led to recommendations about their commonalities and implications (the first chapters of part IV).

PRINCIPLES OF POLICY-MAKING IN EDUCATION

Deriving first from conceptual frameworks for educational planning such as those of Schwab (1964), second from empirical evidence on the rise and fall of cases of policy-making, and third from existing models of policy-making, the following principles are considered crucial to educational policy-making:

1. *An ecological approach to education.* This approach envisions education as a system, a network of interacting factors constituting the context in which education takes place.
2. *A Schwabian orientation to policy-making in education.* Schwab called for the involvement of representatives of different "commonplaces," namely central topics relevant to educational planning, in the processes (see below). This view encompasses the optimal participants, the necessary modes of deliberation, and the need for coordination at many levels.

3. *A view of policy statements as having potential for flexible implementation.* Centrally devised policy might not be suitable for different localities. The notion of "policy potential" in analogy to "curriculum potential" (Ben-Peretz 1990a; see chapter 5), means that policy statements may be adapted to fit specific local contexts. For instance, a policy that requires individual computers for each student in a school setting lacking such physical resources may have to find different ways to introduce students to present-day technology.

These three principles form the basis of my holistic model for policy-making in response to the major dimensions of global change. The proposed model interrelates the three main domains of education and involves representatives of the dimensions of global changes cooperatively in the deliberations that lead to a coordinated policy statement, while leaving freedom for necessary local adaptations. Based on these principles and on this book's prior analysis of concrete cases of policy-making, I suggest the following four major questions that must be addressed in any policy-making model:

- Who will the participants in the process be, as representatives of the "commonplaces" of policy-making?
- Which factors will influence and/or control policy-making?
- What process of policy-making (phases and sequences) will transpire?
- What will be the nature of the final product?

Answers to each of these four questions are furnished by my proposed systemic model.

PARTICIPANTS

Based on the review of existing conceptual frameworks and modes of policy-making and on my personal experience and surveyed empirical evidence, I recommend that the notion of "commonplaces" suggested by Schwab (1964) should be conceived as the basis for appointing appropriate participants to any policy-making committee aiming for educational reform. Schwab's commonplaces for curriculum development are reviewed, followed by an attempt to transfer those curricular concepts to the world of policy-making while incorporating all three domains of education, not just curriculum, and to link the notion of policy commonplaces to the choice of participants.

Effects of Commonplaces on Selection of Curriculum Development Participants

By "commonplaces," Schwab (1964) means those topics and parameters that require attention by planners involved in curriculum development. Schwab suggests the following "commonplaces" for curriculum development: subject matter, learner, teacher, and milieu. Schwab argues that all of these topics must be coordinated so that none is passed by in the process of planning curricula. According to Schwab, any curriculum development group must include representatives of each commonplace, though sometimes one person may represent more than one commonplace.

The "subject matter" commonplace relates to the disciplines and contents to be taught and is obviously of major importance in curriculum development. Thus, for example, in a group developing a new curriculum in history, a historian would be the participant appointed to represent the subject matter commonplace.

Still, Schwab warns that without careful consideration of the nature of the "learner" and "teacher" commonplaces, no valid and effective curricula can be designed. Continuing the history example from above, teachers would participate in the curriculum development group in two capacities: representing the history teacher commonplace, clearly, but also representing the student commonplace in the history class because of teachers' knowledge about students.

The "milieu" commonplace; namely, the physical, social, cultural, and pedagogic environments, renders a major impact on the viability and usability of curricula and must be carefully regarded in the process of curriculum development. Thus, in the example of the new history curriculum, the milieu commonplace may be represented by members of the community who have a special interest in the topics to be studied, for example, Holocaust survivors in a curriculum committee focusing on Holocaust history. As the "milieu" also refers to the physical and economic environment, any curriculum project that requires elaborate laboratories should carefully identify the possibilities for implementation in diverse contexts.

During the curriculum development process, representatives of these four commonplaces interact and deliberate on the desired curriculum in order to reach coordination among diverse points of view. A curriculum product that is the outcome of such deliberation and coordination has the potential for successful implementation in schools. Evading the issue of milieu, for instance, can lead to a curriculum that does not account for necessary physical or social conditions in its design and implementation, which may lead to policy failure.

Effects of Commonplaces on Selection of Policy-Making Participants

Due to the differences between curriculum development and policy-making, the commonplaces suggested by Schwab for the former are not directly applicable to the latter. Curriculum development is only one of the three domains inherent to educational policy-making. The additional educational domains, teaching, and teacher education as well as the need to include representatives of global changes in the deliberations expand the parameters or commonplaces crucial to selecting participant policy makers.

Hence, the following five commonplaces are proposed, herewith, as critical for policy-making in education in light of the three education domains and in response to today's global changes: scientific background, agents, learners, milieu, and media. These five commonplaces of policy-making in education also address various elements mentioned in relation to actual cases of policy-making, as described above in chapter 11. As argued by Schwab on curriculum development, all of these topics should be coordinated in order to facilitate the policy-making process. Like for the case of curriculum development groups, any policy-making group must appoint representatives of each of the five commonplaces, although one person may sometimes represent more than one commonplace.

The "scientific background" commonplace concerns the knowledge base for making decisions about a policy in education that adequately responds to the current effects of globalization and estimates future trends and needs in all four of the globalization dimensions. For instance, the knowledge base related to global warming may lead to a policy decision that assigns priority to this topic and requires its inclusion in education programs from preschool to higher education. Knowledge about immigration is crucial for making decisions about a policy that aims to serve immigrant students. Likewise, without a deep understanding of the globalized economy and its consequences, as well as of the impact of international communication, no relevant and viable policy-making is possible. As a result, any policy-making committee that aims to address global changes must include representatives who possess scientific knowledge in these areas. The scientific background commonplace includes, as well, knowledge and insights gained in the three education domains relevant to policy-making as discussed in part II.

The "agent" or "stakeholder" commonplace covers several important players in the policy field: executives, bureaucrats, educators, parents, as well as organizations like teacher unions and other interest groups (Ben-Peretz 1995a; Grindle 2004; Lo Bianco 2004; Swanson and Barlage 2006). Their interactions, motivations, and power relations are essential determinants in policy-making. A list of potential agents is presented in chapter 11 (see p. 119). The exact nature of representatives for agents depends on their relative power as players in the policy field as well as on the preferences of the powerful people who serve as central decision makers at the inception of the committee, such as the Minister of Education. Because of the power of teacher unions, their representatives are usually included in the policy-making committee. Representatives of teachers are necessary as they have intimate knowledge of classroom situations and represent one of the three relevant domains of education.

The "learner" commonplace, referring to students' cultural background, age, and knowledge base, must be accounted for in the process of policy-making. Learners cannot be considered passive recipients of policy decisions. In curriculum development, as envisioned by Schwab (1964), the nature of diverse target populations of learners has to be considered and weighed carefully. This situation is exacerbated in times of massive demographic movements and requires thoughtful attention by policy makers. For policy-making in response to global changes, a representative of the learner commonplace may actually represent target populations outside schools, such as adult learning institutions or other target populations in the general public. Representatives of "learners" could be high school or university students but also could be members of adult education groups.

The "milieu" commonplace is an important component in any attempt to plan and implement policy. Milieu is a composite of various parameters in the social and physical realm. The milieu of policy-making includes the economic situation, how pressing the economic concerns are in a globalized economy, and whether the economy enables policy makers to realize their intentions. Another important feature of milieu is the political climate. The political climate, both before or after elections, might have an impact on the motivation of political figures to initiate, and sometimes to prevent, policy ventures. The cultural environment, as well, is meaningful for policy-making.

Policy-making does not occur in a void but rather is embedded in a specific social and cultural context that both extends and limits its scope. For example, a highly traditional society might welcome policy emphasizing the cultivation of traditional values and may strongly oppose more innovative approaches. In policy-making, one also must consider the *zeitgeist*, the present-day trends that influence the nature of policies. Beyond the social and cultural aspects of milieu, there may also be physical aspects of certain environments that impact policy-making. Thus, the absence of computers in schools restricts any attempts to plan an agenda of computerized teaching and learning. Very crowded living conditions may stimulate a policy of providing children with public spaces that compensate for their difficult home situations. Representatives of milieu could be leaders in the economy, both as "consumers" of schooling and as experts in the needs of the globalized economy or experts on the physical conditions of schools. Scholars in political science could represent political cultural issues.

The "media" commonplace constitutes a novel commonplace in educational planning. In the changing world of the twenty-first century, media are active players in policy-making. Written, oral, and visual texts lucidly voice a range of concerns, critiques, and proposed agendas, thereby demanding the attention of policy makers. For instance, a television program aired on prime time that focuses on the suffering of immigrants may create such public backlash that policy makers strengthen their efforts to provide appropriate schooling to immigrant students. Newspaper reports on the performance of students in international evaluation endeavors are very powerful in shaping public opinion concerning appropriate policies. Media also play a role in educating the general public. For instance, television or newspaper exposés may be used to educate citizens about water shortages and ways to conserve water. Journalists or producers in television, as well as scholars in the media domain, could act as representatives of this commonplace.

A crucial issue in policy-making concerns the political appointment of these representatives. Empirical evidence, such as the Grindle (2004) study and the Israeli experience (Ben-Peretz 1995a) reported in chapter 11, shows that political power plays a central role in policy-making, including the appointment of participants in the process. If the representatives are mostly political appointments, it might be difficult for these different commonplaces to interact freely and constructively to obtain the necessary coordination and mutual recognition during the process of policy-making and to achieve successful, positive outcomes. It is important for the participants to be confident in voicing their opinions, as the Director of the Ministry of Education suggested in the case of reform in teacher education in Israel, reported in chapter 9 (p. 94). The coordination among diverse voices is crucial for reaching an integrated and holistic policy response to global changes.

The principles of commonplaces in policy-making in education in response to global changes are congruent with some of the empirical evidence presented above in several cases of policy-making. In these cases, such as shown in chapters 8 and 9, interplay emerges among diverse agents who are central players in the field; moreover, conflicts and opposition arise. Some of these agents, like representatives of governmental bureaucracy such as the Ministry of Education or representatives of teacher unions, may be especially powerful in determining outcomes of the policy-making process. In this sense, the agent commonplace here may overlap with the influential organizations and influential people mentioned in the Swanson and Barlage study (2006).

The most effective means for coping with the power imbalance between different participants in the policy-making committee may lie in the actual process of group deliberations, as it unfolds. Gradually, more representatives of each commonplace may be drawn into the deliberations of the group. According to Schwab, these deliberations might lead to mutual recognition of the validity of arguments, and finally, to a measure of co-ordination and consensus among the diverse interests represented in the group. Thus, deliberations among the influential and not-so-influential participants constitute a critical phase in the development from a mere policy initiative to a shared policy document.

FACTORS THAT INFLUENCE AND/OR CONTROL POLICY-MAKING

In summarizing the empirical data and based on my personal experience chairing reform committees, it seems that two central factors influence, and sometimes even control, policy-making. These dual factors, power relations and time, must both be considered in any systemic, holistic model for policy-making.

Power Relations

Power represents the ability of different participants to enforce their views on the process of policy-making. The use of power may be positive, aiming to promote policy agendas, or may be negative, intending to prevent the policy from progressing. Power is an elusive concept; it may be institutional—part of the mandate of an organization like the national parliament, or of a person like the Minister of Education. Power may also be a personal quality—the charismatic or manipulative abilities of a person, like individual scientists, teachers, or parents. Power is also a quality emerging from the combined pressure of a group of people like a teacher union.

During any process of policy-making, the power factor plays a central role and must be considered. An interesting aspect of power relations concerns the interplay between individuals and associations or communities. Ben-Peretz (2003) shows a seesaw balance between two different power agents—the Minister of Education and the teacher unions or universities—in the matriculation policy reform committee described in chapter 8. In an article on the life cycles of reforms, Ben-Peretz (2008) claims:

> Power may be held by individuals, like Ministers of Education, by prominent politicians, or by the media. On the other hand, there are groups, such as teacher organizations, parents or religious institutions, and industry sectors

that voice their strong commitments. The outcomes of the power relations between these forces may determine the path taken by the education establishment. Sometimes a strong and powerful Minister of Education can impose his or her ideas about the appropriate policy on the system (Ben-Peretz 2008, 9).

This balance changed when efforts to implement the new policy ceased after elections, because a new Minister of Education was appointed:

> The seesaw mode of initiation and implementation of educational reform is related to the changing balance between the power of individuals and other forces. Ministers of Education are not the only individuals whose personal power has far reaching consequences on education reform. Chairpersons of school boards, dominant principals or influential schools might initiate school reform. Yet in every case one has to reckon as well with the forces that play a role in the specific context of the reform, and might cause the seesaw effect described above (Ben-Peretz 2003, 55).

The changing power relations among participants often lead to the abandoning of a policy and to its reappearance after some time, revealing a phenomenon where trends in education cause the field to adopt, reject, and readopt reform movements.

> This bandwagon nature of educational reform seems to highlight the central and crucial role played by individuals, and political parties, in positions of power. On the other hand, it is important to remember the origin of the matriculation reform in social and pedagogical problems associated with the existing situation. These problems did not vanish with election outcomes. Moreover, the brief period of courageous attempts to introduce radical changes in the existing state of affairs left its mark on the system, so that with some slight encouragement parts of the matriculation reform seem to get another chance. The outcomes of this reawakening are not yet clear but it demonstrates the complexity of interactions and power relations between individuals and societal forces inherent in any effort to introduce changes into an educational system (Ben-Peretz 2003, 52–53).

Temporal Issues

Studies on policy-making have shown that time is also a crucial factor in the process. First, timing the initiation of a new policy process may determine its success or failure. The saying "the time is ripe" for a certain action is certainly relevant here. Research has tried to determine the influence of certain political events, like elections, on policy initiatives in education. Grindle (2004) claims that initiatives during elections do not seem to have an impact on election outcomes. Still, Vanhuysse and Sulitzeanu-Kenan (in press) claim that: "When bureaucratic principals need to be elected, voting and unionization are both likely to further increase the power of bureaucratic agents." They argue that issues of timing and power relations concerning reforms in education require in-depth studies.

Time plays another role in policy-making related to questions like the optimal length of time for planning activities during the committee's work or the time gap between planning and implementing policy (Ben-Peretz 1990b; Grindle 2004).

The time and power factors are fluid and interact with each other. Ministerial power determines timing, whereas strong unions may cause long delays in the process. It seems that policies of reform have a life cycle that determines their development and decline (Ben-Peretz 2008). The metaphor of a life cycle views the history of reform through the biological lens of birth, growth, and decline. The cycle metaphor as relevant to reform movements can appear at two levels: the life cycle of specific reform ventures, such as initiating a national curriculum, and the cyclic appearance of innovative structural or pedagogical reforms, representing the phenomenon of reform in general.

THE PROPOSED SYSTEMIC, HOLISTIC MODEL FOR POLICY-MAKING IN RESPONSE TO GLOBAL CHANGES

I move now to the model proposed in this book, which is intended for policy-making on a national level. Figure 13.1 shows a visual representation of the proposed holistic model.

The process of policy-making envisioned herewith is characterized by several features. This process is

- *Modular*—divided into distinct parts that may be dealt with separately and integrated later on. For instance, different panels and subcommittees that are organized during the deliberation phases may work independently and share their work whenever this is considered appropriate.
- *Layered*—each phase of the process constitutes one layer.
- *Sequential*—the diverse layers have a predetermined sequence.
- *Communal*—the process depends on interaction and coordination reflecting a "rainbow coalition" of voices (Nicholson 1989).
- *Spiral*—policy-making is envisioned as moving hierarchically, culminating in the highest level of policy formulation.

Participants in the process are conceived as representing the aforementioned "commonplaces" of policy-making, namely: scientific background, agents, learners, milieu, and media. Because of the manifold aspects of

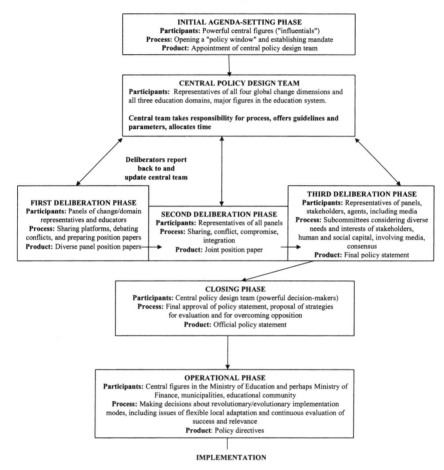

INITIAL AGENDA-SETTING PHASE
Participants: Powerful central figures ("influentials")
Process: Opening a "policy window" and establishing mandate
Product: Appointment of central policy design team

CENTRAL POLICY DESIGN TEAM
Participants: Representatives of all four global change dimensions and all three education domains, major figures in the education system.

Central team takes responsibility for process, offers guidelines and parameters, allocates time

**Deliberators report
back to and
update central team**

FIRST DELIBERATION PHASE
Participants: Panels of change/domain representatives and educators
Process: Sharing platforms, debating conflicts, and preparing position papers
Product: Diverse panel position papers

SECOND DELIBERATION PHASE
Participants: Representatives of all panels
Process: Sharing, conflict, compromise, integration
Product: Joint position paper

THIRD DELIBERATION PHASE
Participants: Representatives of panels, stakeholders, agents, including media
Process: Subcommittees considering diverse needs and interests of stakeholders, human and social capital, involving media, consensus
Product: Final policy statement

CLOSING PHASE
Participants: Central policy design team (powerful decision-makers)
Process: Final approval of policy statement, proposal of strategies for evaluation and for overcoming opposition
Product: Official policy statement

OPERATIONAL PHASE
Participants: Central figures in the Ministry of Education and perhaps Ministry of Finance, municipalities, educational community
Process: Making decisions about revolutionary/evolutionary implementation modes, including issues of flexible local adaptation and continuous evaluation of success and relevance
Product: Policy directives

IMPLEMENTATION

Note. The policy-making proposal advanced herewith is complex and time-consuming, but it is conceived as a prerequisite for valid, holistic, synergic, and viable policy-making in response to global changes

Figure 13.1.   Proposed Model of Holistic Policy-Making in Response to Global Changes

"scientific background" and the large number of "agents," for instance, it is inconceivable to place all of them in a common deliberation site. Therefore, several phases of the policy-making process are proposed, reflecting the layered and modular nature of this model of policy-making.

Initiation Phase

The initiation phase determines the policy's fate to a large extent. According to the experience of the policy-making cases reported above, powerful political figures are the most successful initiators (Ben-Peretz 1995a; Grindle 2004). Initiators are responsible for appointing a central policy design team. The initiators generally are powerful central figures, such as Ministers of Education; sometimes these might be prime ministers or presidents.

In the specific case of policy-making that targets appropriate responses to global changes, the first team to be appointed should include representatives of each of the three domains of education—curriculum, teaching, and teacher education, as well as representatives of each area of global change discussed in part I. These participants represent the scientific background commonplace. A major figure in the education system, such as the Director of the Curriculum Department, or one of the general Deputy Directors of the Ministry of Education, should be appointed by the initiator to act as chairperson of the central team. The chair of the central team does not necessarily represent the Ministry of Education. A scholar in education may fulfill this role, as I did in the cases presented in chapters 8 and 9. The number of members in the central team should not exceed eleven: one member for each domain of education and one for each of the global changes, the chairperson, and possibly two or three other influential people, such as scholars in education or the chairperson of the Education Committee in Parliament and possibly an expert on time in schools.

The central team should take responsibility for all further phases of the policy-making process and for the approval of the final document. In order to fulfill this role, they must receive updated information about every phase of deliberation from each subcommittee. The arrows in figure 1 represent this feedback role. The leading team is also responsible for the time allocation of each phase.

First Deliberation Phase

In this phase, which is chaired by one of the members of the central team, several panels are formed independently of the central team. Each panel consists of representatives of one of the dimensions of globalization alongside educators and other experts, who meet to discuss implications for education. Each panel may find it necessary to invite additional members to its deliberations; for instance, in the immigration panel, sociologists who are knowledgeable about migration may wish to include historians in order to gain insights into the nature of international migration.

The educators participating in each panel are conceived as experts in the three domains: curriculum, teaching, and teacher education. In the deliberations of each panel, a curriculum expert might refer to existing curricular materials or may suggest guidelines for developing new curricula. An expert on teaching may present problems ensuing from teachers' views and self-images, whereas an expert in teacher education might discuss the possible impact of a new policy on teacher education programs. These educators may represent, as well, the learner commonplace due to their intimate knowledge of educational situations, in and out of schools. As stated in chapter 3, p. 26, concerning technology education policy has to address three outcomes important for citizens: skills, problem-solving capacity, and a set of values. It is the role of educators in the deliberation phases to consider these outcomes in relation to all global issues.

The panels should consider past, present, and future problems likely to be elicited by each of the global issues at hand as well as programs that were devised in an attempt to address these issues. Panels should discuss unique problems in the field that may be elicited by educating students about global changes as well as guidelines for a globally accountable educational plan and ways to evaluate its success.

Each panel should have a precise timetable for its work and should prepare a position paper that sums up its deliberations. An example of such a position paper in the immigration dimension could include, for instance, recommendations about creating special education opportunities for parents of migrant students in the form of community schools. The technology panel could possibly recommend large-scale teacher inservice education programs for promoting the use of the information highway in schools. The panel dealing with economic globalization might wish to introduce a nationwide plan for identifying students with scientific abilities at a very early age in order to provide them with appropriate education opportunities, using institutions of higher education as well as industry and corporations. The environment panel might advocate including a special school subject called Environment from kindergarten onward.

The holistic approach to policy-making advocated in this book calls for the coordination of different dimensions of globalization and for the integration of relevant domains of education. The first deliberation phase provides each global change dimension with space for presenting its case and for considering the implications for education. Each panel creates its own position paper. These diverse position papers should be shared and coordinated among the panels, in the second phase of deliberations. The sharing of position papers reflects the communal aspect of the proposed process.

Second Deliberation Phase

The purpose of this phase, chaired by a member of the central team, is to integrate the diverse position papers that focused on each of the global change dimensions. In order to create a manageable and interactive deliberation group, each of the panels in the first deliberation phase sends two members to the joint panel. At this stage, it is important, for instance, to consider the impact of migration on issues of environmental education or to keep in mind technological advances and their potential meanings for education projects.

The joint panel includes representatives of each of the three domains of education: curriculum, teaching, and teacher education. The role of representatives of these three domains is to suggest the possible significance of the evolving policy on curriculum development, the role of teachers, and on teacher education programs. For instance, creating an integrative, interdisciplinary environmental education plan may require changes in curriculum, teaching, and teacher education. The question of financial and political support of new educational plans should also be addressed in this phase in order to include the milieu commonplace within the considerations leading to viable policy.

The time allocation for this phase is longer than for that for the first phase, as conflicts might arise among representatives of the various global dimension panels and educational domains who participate in the deliberations. A member of the Central Team is needed as chair to support the process and document its advancement. At the end of this phase, a joint position paper is drafted for the next sequence, when several stakeholders are introduced into the process.

Third Deliberation Phase

This stage of the policy-making process, chaired, as well, by a member of the Central Team, uses as its starting point the existing joint position paper, which represents previous modular deliberations and the tentative consensus reached in the integration of diverse platforms by representatives of the various global dimensions and educational domains. This paper now serves as the starting point for deliberations involving presenters of the joint position paper, along with stakeholders like representatives of teacher organizations, principals, teachers, parents, political leaders, and other members of the community. These participants represent the commonplace "agents" and "learners."

It is especially important at this stage to include the voices of minority communities and immigrants. Representatives of the media commonplace may assist the participants in forming a policy that is sufficiently powerful to reach people and gain their support. As mentioned in the analysis of the policy-making cases in part III, a policy must have widespread political agreement in order to exert the influence that can lead to its successful implementation. Because of the large number of participants in this phase, subcommittees must be formed to share their insights with the whole group, following the examples of the Israeli Committee on Teacher Education (chapter 9).

One example of a subcommittee might focus on the possible impact of new policy on schools. Such a subcommittee could include principals, teachers, representatives of teacher organizations, and parents as well as advocates of the policy itself. Another subcommittee might focus on issues of target populations. Such a subcommittee could include representatives of higher education and adult education institutes as well as representatives of minority or migrant populations. The role of such a subcommittee would be to provide insights into the needs of multiple populations in the context of the policy.

The product of the third phase of deliberations is a final policy statement that specifies goals as well as strategies for implementation, including financial implications, suggestions for curriculum development, proposed modes of teaching, and recommended preservice and inservice teacher education programs, which all play integral roles in the policy statement.

The time necessary for completing the three deliberation phases may range between a year to a year-and-a-half. This was approximately the time required for reaching joint recommendations in the cases presented in part III.

Closing Phase

At this stage of policy-making, the policy statement is returned to the Central Design team for final approval. It is important that at this stage representatives of powerful decision makers are among the participants. Implementation of any new policy requires close evaluation to ensure its validity. Therefore, it is important that at the closing phase the Central Design Team proposes some evaluation strategies. The closing phase is also the time for weighing priorities among the different parts of the policy and finding ways to overcome opposition. At this stage of policy-making, political considerations may come into the foreground, and the policy must be justified from various points of view. Coalitions might be formed in order to ensure widespread support for the policy. Financial issues, as well as timing, must be carefully considered.

The final policy document sets priorities among the different recommendations, and it specifies responsibilities for carrying out these recommendations. See the Appendix for some concrete examples of the committee's recommendations for matriculation examinations, as stated in the final document (based on the case presented in chapter 8).

Operational Phase

This is obviously a crucial phase for any endeavor of policy-making. Decisions about implementation modes must be made, for instance, in choosing revolutionary or evolutionary modes as described in chapter 8. A revolutionary implementation mode is based on the power of decision makers to enforce the new policy by a top-down decree. Such is the case of the introduction of junior high schools in Israel. An evolutionary mode relies on grassroot experiences in implementing the new policy, like the twenty-two high schools involved in implementing the new matriculation policy in Israel.

A search for optimal synergy among the various agents involved in implementing educational reform is vital for the policy's success. Synergy is the coordination and combination of many factors, which collectively yield a larger sum than their parts, leading to mutually reinforcing and to cumulative results. In the case of the Israeli junior high school reform (see chapter 10), the many factors included (a) central and local authorities, (b) stakeholders, and (c) factors external to the school system:

> The changing interactions between these factors may be seen to promote, or otherwise, hinder the implementation of school reform policies. It is contended that the complex interaction of the many factors involved yields results which cannot be accounted for by simply weighing the potential impact of each factor by itself (Ben-Peretz 1997, 8).

Powerful decision makers make issues of flexible local adaptations that reflect the "policy potential" at this stage. As stated previously, not every general policy decision is necessarily suitable for diverse locations and contexts. So, for example, the general policy recommendations of the matriculation committee in Israel to reduce the number of external examinations required adaptation to the needs of religious communities, where specific religious subject-matter disciplines had to be added to the list of compulsory matriculation examinations. As stated in chapter 1 (p. 7), there are profound differences between macro trends in education and their local manifestations requiring appropriate accommodation.

Spiral Features, Power Relations, and Time in Policy-Making

Three major aspects of the proposed policy-making model deserve some elaboration.

Spiral policy. The final policy statement arrived at in the third phase of deliberations is conceived as the culmination of a spiral process that started with appointing a Central Design Team and that evolved through different phases of deliberations. In an analogy to the spiral curriculum, which according to Bruner (1960, 1996) is built upon previous learning experiences and eventually reaches the highest level of abstraction, the spiral policy reaches the highest level of specification of goals and strategies for policy in education, building on the previous phases of deliberation. At the highest part of the spiral, the policy statement is returned to the Central Design Team for final approval (in the closing phase) and for ministerial decisions about implementation modes (in the operational phase).

Crucial roles of power relations and time in policy-making. The terms *power positions* and *timing* reappear in all analyses of policy-making in education, and as well in the model proposed herewith. Powerful figures are usually initiators of policy-making, and they determine its fate. In this context, it is important to note the seesaw relationship that might exist between powerful individuals, on the one hand, and the societal pressure groups, on the other hand, in democratic regimes. Even when individuals change, like presidents or Ministers of Education, and reforms seem to decline and even disappear, the needs and voices of community groups might regain their influence and cause a cyclic reappearance of policy endeavors. These cycles were discussed above (in chapter 8 and in this chapter). Moreover, as shown in the analysis of cases of policy-making (part III), and of the general societal impact of globalization (part I), international movements and nongovernmental organizations can have a powerful influence in many countries.

While "power" is a naturally accepted component of policy-making, "time" is a more elusive concept in this context. Yet, it plays a crucial role in policy-making and implementation as was discussed previously, relating to the timing of policy-making (chapter 12). In the process of policy design, the importance of using time wisely cannot be overstated. Time schedules must be specified, and efforts should be made to adhere to them. Nonetheless, sometimes unexpected time is required for the complex process of coordinating among diverse platforms and for dealing with conflict situations. Policy-making has a better chance for success if participants in the different phases of deliberations form, over time, a community with shared goals. Thus, the spiral policy might reach its highest level.

Because of the modular, layered, and sequential characteristics of the proposed model, there may be time gaps between different phases of deliberations, caused by the interaction of power relations and timing considerations. Thus, central decision makers may consider it necessary to postpone the third deliberation phase until a more supportive political climate is available.

CONCLUDING COMMENTS

This last chapter presents the proposed holistic model for policy-making in education in response to global changes. This model incorporates the diverse contributions of representatives of global changes, and domains of education, as well as the voices of other agents and stakeholders in a complicated process. The process includes several layers, phases that are organized in a predetermined sequence, culminating in an official policy statement at the highest level of the spiral of policy development. The model is conceived to lead to general recommendations, involving changes in curriculum, teaching, and teacher education, but it affords local administration the power to adapt these recommendations to their specific contexts. Synergy among different parties and factors is crucial for the success of the new policies.

Epilogue

The journey undertaken in this book has come to its end. I started with an overview of dramatic and overriding global changes that call for appropriate and timely responses by the education system. I suggested that an adequate response to globalization challenges requires a holistic approach to several different dimensions—immigration, technology, economy, environment—as well as effective collaboration and coordination among the central domains of education: curriculum, teaching, and teacher education. The second part of the book analyzed relevant literature in education and its implications for policy-making. Several cases of policy-making were presented in the third part in order to elicit common features of this process as guidelines for the holistic policy-making model proposed in the last part of this book.

Along the way, I became more and more aware of the double-headed nature of globalization, like Janus of Roman mythology. On the one hand, globalization might, and does, provide incentives for economic advancement and for large-scale scientific development. In this role, it figures as a catalyst for profound societal transformations. The rapid development of India is a prime example of this generous influence of globalization. On the other hand, rapid economic development is accompanied by far-reaching negative and even dangerous alterations in the environment. Moreover, the positive impact of economic and technological changes exacerbates divisions between the "haves" and the "have-nots," between producers and consumers, between developed and underdeveloped countries. The trend for "self-serving diversity" might be conceived as the writing on the wall, warning everyone that the future of humanity is at stake now.

As educational policy makers stand at the entrance to the unknown passageway leading toward global changes and transitions, they symbolize the progression of past into future, of one vision to another. Globalization faces us with the mistakes and successes of the past and presents, at the same time, hope for a brighter future while summoning up realistic forecasts. It is the role of educators to respond to these challenges by raising public awareness about the vast array of potentials, as well as the inherent dangers, of globalization for the citizens of the twenty-first century.

It is my hope that this book, its rationale, and the holistic model for policy-making in education that it proposes, will serve educators, policy makers, and leaders to navigate valid, effective, and comprehensive responses in coping with the difficult and complex issues elicited by present-day global changes.

Appendix

CONCRETE EXAMPLES OF RECOMMENDATIONS BY THE
POLICY COMMITTEE FOR MATRICULATION EXAMINATIONS,
AS STATED IN THE FINAL POLICY DOCUMENT REPORT *

1) **Main recommendations**

— Curricula and achievement tests should be organized in three modular levels: basic, regular, and advanced. Each subject matter and level should contain one questionnaire.
— The final assessments should be in two formats: external and school-based. The grades in the Matriculation Certificate should not distinguish between the two formats.
— In the first implementation stage (see below for timing), three subject-matter discipline grades, out of the nine required for matriculation, should be school-based. In the final implementation stage, six subject-matter grades should be school-based.
— The right of the school to grant school-based grades must be approved by the Ministry of Education.
— The Ministry of Education decides on compulsory and elective subject-matter disciplines.
— Matriculation examinations should be adapted to the religious-cultural needs of specific populations: Muslims, Druze, Jewish ultra-orthodox, and so on.
— Diverse modes of evaluation should be included in assessments of achievement, such as project work, portfolios, etc.

---

* Israel Ministry of Education, Culture, and Sport (1994). See also chapter 8.

153

2) Specific responsibilities for carrying out these recommendations

— Establishing a guidance and supervision agency; creating special centers for teacher development in the field of measurement and assessment.
— Improving teaching facilities, such as libraries and information networks.
— Ensuring the status and work conditions of teachers in senior high schools.
— Accompanying the change process with formative and summative evaluation strategies.
— Allocating necessary financial resources for implementing the policy recommendations.

3) Stages of implementation

— First stage: 1st–3rd year
— Second stage: 4th–5th year

The committee recommends that after five years, the Ministry of Education should conclude the implementation process.

References

Anderson, L. W. 1985. Time and timing. Eds. C. W. Fisher and D. C. Berliner. *Perspectives on instructional time*. New York: Longman, 157–68.

Anyon, J. 1981. Social class and school knowledge. *Curriculum Inquiry* 11: 3–42.

Apple, M. W., J. Kenway, and M. Singh. 2007. *Globalizing education: Policies, pedagogies, & politics*. New York: Peter Lang.

Archibugi, D., and C. Pietrobelli. 2003. The globalisation of technology and its implications for developing countries: Windows of opportunity or further burden? *Technological Forecasting and Social Change* 70: 861–83.

Babylon Online Dictionary. Retrieved on June 15, 2008: http://dictionary.babylon. com/.

Banathy, B. H. 1996. Systems inquiry and its application in education. Ed. D. H. Jonassen. *Handbook of Research for Educational Communication and Technology*. New York: Macmillan Library Reference USA, 74–92.

Bandura, A. 1977. *Social learning theory*. Englewood Cliffs, NJ: Prentice-Hall.

Barab, S. A., and W. M. Roth. 2006. Curriculum-based ecosystems: Supporting knowing from an ecological perspective. *Educational Researcher* 35(5): 3–13.

Barnum, C., and N. Walniansky. 1989. Globalization: Moving a step beyond the international firm. *Management Review* 78(9): 30.

Barr, R., and C. Lacey. 1998. Immigration and education: Issues and research report. *Executive Summary: The Spencer Foundation*. Retrieved March 3, 2008: http://www. spencer.org/publications/conferences/Immigration/report.htm.

Bazalgette, C. 1989. *Primary media education: A curriculum statement*. London: British Film Institute.

Beck, U. 2000. The cosmopolitan perspective: Sociology of the second age of modernity. *British Journal of Sociology* 51(1): 79–105.

Beijaard, D., N. Verloop, and J. D. Vermunt. 2000. Teachers' perceptions of professional identity: An exploratory study from a personal knowledge perspective. *Teaching and Teacher Education* 16(7): 749–64.

Ben-Peretz, M. 1980. Environmental education is too important to be left in the hands of teachers alone. Eds. T. S. Bakshi and Z. Naveh. *Environmental education: Principles, methods and applications.* New York: Plenum Press, 19–30.

———. 1990a. *The teacher-curriculum encounter: Freeing teachers from the tyranny of texts.* Albany: SUNY Press.

———. 1990b. Perspectives on time in education. Eds. M. Ben-Peretz and R. Bromme. *The nature of time in schools: Theoretical concepts, practitioner perceptions.* New York and London: Teachers College Press, Columbia University, 64–77.

———. 1995a. Educational reform in Israel: An example of synergy in education. Eds. D. S. G. Carter and M. H. O'Neill. *Case studies in educational change: An international perspective.* London: The Falmer Press, 86–95.

———. 1995b. The impact of teaching situations on teachers' memory (chapter 4). Ed. M. Ben-Peretz. *Learning from experience: Memory and the teacher's account of teaching.* New York: State University Press, 45–62.

———. 1995c. Systemic reform in national assessments: The determination of policy and its relation to practice. Paper presented at the European Conference on Educational Research, University of Bath, England, September.

———. 1996. Culture and ideology: The development of a national curriculum in Israel. Paper presented at the Society for the Study of Curriculum History, Culture and Ideology, New York.

———. 1997. Review: The quest for utopia: Social ideologies and the curriculum. *American Journal of Education* 105(4): 437–45.

———. 1999. The politics of education and the future of teaching. *Teaching and Teacher Education* 15(8): 951–55.

———. 2000. When teaching changes, can teacher education be far behind? *Prospects* 30(2): 215–24.

———. 2001. The impossible role of teacher educators in a changing world. *Journal of Teacher Education* 52(1): 48–56.

———. 2003. Curriculum reform in Israel: The power of individuals and other forces. Eds. J. van den Akker, U. Hameyer, and W. A. J. M. Kuiper. *Curriculum landscapes and trends.* The Netherlands: Kluwer, 45–59.

———. 2008. *The lifecycle of reform in education from the circumstances of birth to the stages of decline: Causes, ideologies and power relations.* Based on an Inaugural Lecture delivered at the Institute of Education, University of London, June 19, 2007. London: Institute of Education, University of London.

Ben-Peretz, M., and B. Eilam. In press. Curriculum use in the classroom. Eds. E. Baker, B. McGaw, and P. Peterson. *International encyclopaedia of education, third edition.* Oxford: Elsevier.

Ben-Peretz, M., and I. Kupferberg. 2007. Does teachers' negotiation of personal cases in an interactive cyber forum contribute to their professional learning? *Teachers and Teaching: Theory and Practice* 13(2): 125–43.

Ben-Peretz, M., and R. Lotan. In press. Social and cultural influences on teacher education. Eds. E. Baker, B. McGaw, and P. Peterson. *International encyclopedia of education, third edition.* Oxford: Elsevier.

Ben-Peretz, M., N. Mendelson, and F. W. Kron. 2003. How teachers in different educational contexts view their roles. *Teaching and Teacher Education* 19: 277–90, chapter 10.

Ben-Peretz, M., and M. Silberstein. 1982. *A curriculum development case study in biology: Two levels of interpretations.* Jerusalem: Ministry of Education and Culture.

Ben-Peretz, M., and A. Zajdman. 1986. Three generations of school curriculum development in Israel. *Studies in Education* 43–44: 317–27 (in Hebrew).

Berlak, A., and H. Berlak. 1977. On the uses of social psychological research on schooling. Essay review of *Beyond surface curriculum: An interview study of teachers' understandings.* Eds. A. M. Bussis, E. A. Chittenden, and M. Amarel. Boulder, CO: Westview Press, 1976 in *School Review* 85(4): 577–88.

Beyer, L. E., and D. P. Liston. 1996. *Curriculum in conflict: Social visions, educational agendas, and progressive school reform.* New York: Teachers College Press.

Bhagwati, J. N. 2002. Coping with antiglobalization: A trilogy of discontents. *Foreign Affairs* 81(1): 2.

Bishop, J. H. 1990. The productivity consequences of what is learned in high school. *Journal of Curriculum Studies* 22(2): 101–26.

Boyd-Barrett, O. 2000. The new environment of media education. Eds. B. Moon, S. Brown, and M. Ben-Peretz. *Routledge international companion to education.* New York and London: Routledge, 513–29.

Brennan, M. J. 1974. Total education for the total environment. *Journal of Environmental Education* 6(1): 16–19.

Bruner, J. 1960. *The process of education.* Cambridge, MA: Harvard University Press.

———. 1996. *The culture of education.* Cambridge, MA: Harvard University Press.

Burbules, N. C., and C. A. Torres. 2000. *Globalization and education: Critical perspectives.* New York and London: Routledge.

Burbules, N. C., and C. A. Torres. 2000. Globalization and education: An introduction. Eds. N. C. Burbules and C. A. Torres. *Globalization and education: Critical perspectives.* New York: Routledge, 1–26.

Caldwell, L. K. 2005. International environmental policy. Eds. B. Mazlish and A. Iriye. *The global history reader.* New York: Routledge, 146–56.

Castells, M. 1996. *The rise of the network society.* Oxford: Blackwell.

———. 1999. Information technology, globalization and social development. United Nations Research Institute for Social Development (UNRISD) Discussion paper No. 114, September.

Chanda, N. 2007. *Bound together.* New York: Yale University Press.

Cheng, K. M. 1997. What have been reformed? A review of two decades' reform in China's education. Paper presented at the Oxford International Conference in Education and Development, "Education and Geopolitical Change," September 11–15, New College, Oxford.

Cho, E. K., and S. Shin. 2008. Survival, adjustment, and acculturation of newly immigrated families with school-age children: Cases of four Korean families. *Diaspora, Indigenous and Minority Education: An International Journal* 2(1): 4–24.

Chronaki, A. 2000. Computers in classrooms: Learners and teachers in new roles. Eds. B. Moon, S. Brown, and M. Ben-Peretz. *Routledge international companion to education.* New York: Routledge, 558–72.

Cochran-Smith, M. 2000. Teacher education at the turn of the century [editorial]. *Journal of Teacher Education* 51(3): 163–65.

Cochran-Smith, M., and K. M. Zeichner. 2005. Studying teacher education: The report of the AERA panel on research and teacher education. Washington, D.C.: The American Educational Research Association.

Cohen, R. 2005. Diasporas, the nation state, and globalization. Eds. B. Mazlish and A. Iriye. *The global history reader.* New York: Routledge, 92–103.

Coleman, J. S. 1988. Social capital in the creation of human capital. *American Journal of Sociology* (Supplement) S95–S120.

Connelly, F. M. 1972. The functions of curriculum development. *Interchange* 3(2–3): 161–77.

———. 1995. Forward in M. Ben-Peretz. *Learning from experience: Memory and the teacher's account of teaching.* New York: State University Press, xiii–xviii.

Connelly, F. M., and D. J. Clandinin. 1988. *Teachers as curriculum planners: Narratives of experience.* New York: Teachers College Press and Toronto: OISE Press.

Conway, M. A. 1990. *Autobiographical memory: An introduction.* Philadelphia: Open University Press.

Dar, Y., and N. Resh. 1988. Educational integration and scholastic achievement: A summary and evaluation of research in Israel. *Megamot* 31(2): 180–207 (in Hebrew).

Darling-Hammond, L. 2006. Constructing 21st-century teacher education. *Journal of Teacher Education* 57(3): 300–314.

de Vries, M. J. 2000. Technology education: Towards a new school subject. Eds. B. Moon, S. Brown, and M. Ben-Peretz. *Routledge international companion to education.* New York: Routledge, 910–20.

Delors, J. 1996. Learning: The treasure within. Report to UNESCO of International Commission on Education for the Twenty-first Century. Paris: UNESCO.

Dooge, J. C. I. 1996. Policy responses to global environmental issues: An introductory overview. Eds. R. E. Munn, J. W. M. la Riviere, and N. Van Lookeren Campagne. *Policy making in an era of global environment change.* Netherlands: Kluwer Academic, 97–112.

Eden, S. 1991. *Curriculum development.* Jerusalem: The Ministry of Education and Culture.

Eisikovits, R. A. 2008. Coping with high-achieving transnationalist immigrant students: The experience of Israeli teachers. *Teaching and Teacher Education* 24: 277–89.

Elliott, J. 1999. Editorial: Introduction: Global and local dimensions of reforms in teacher education. *Teaching and Teacher Education* 15(2): 133–41.

Encyclopedia Britannica Online. 2008. Retrieved June 15, 2008–2009: www.britannica.com.

Feiman-Nemser, S. 2001. From preparation to practice: Designing a continuum to strengthen and sustain teaching. *Teachers College Record* 103(6): 1013–55.

Fenstermacher, G. D. 1985. Time as the terminus of teaching: A philosophical perspective. Eds. C. W. Fisher and D. C. Berliner. *Perspectives on instructional time.* New York: Longman, 97–108.

Flores, M. A., and C. Day. 2006. Contexts which shape and reshape new teachers' identities: A multi-perspective study. *Teaching and Teacher Education* 22(2): 219–32.

Fullan, M. 1982. *The meaning of educational change*. New York: Teachers College Press.

Geyer, M., and C. Bright. 2005. World history in a global age. Eds. B. Mazlish and A. Iriye. *The global history reader*. New York: Routledge, 21–29.

Gibson, K. 2008. Technology and technological knowledge: A challenge for school curricula. *Teachers and Teaching: Theory and Practice* 14(1): 3–16.

Ginsburg, M. B. 1991. Preface. *Understanding educational reform in global context: Economy, ideology and the state*. New York: Garland Publishing, xv–xx.

Goodlad, J. 1990. *Teachers for our nation's schools*. San Francisco: Jossey-Bass.

Goodlad, J. I., M. Klein, and K. Tye. 1979. The domain of curriculum and their study. Eds. J. I. Goodlad, M. P. Ammons, E. A. Buchanan, E. A. Griffin, G. A. Hill, H. W. Iwanska. *Curriculum inquiry: The study of curriculum practice*. New York: McGraw-Hill, 43–76.

Grant, T., and G. Littlejohn. (Eds.) 2001. *Teaching about climate change: Cool schools tackle global warming*. Canada: New Society.

Grindle, M. S. 2004. *Despite the odds: The contentious politics of education reform*. Princeton: Princeton University Press.

Gungwu, W. 2005. Migration and its enemies. Eds. B. Mazlish and A. Iriye. *The global history reader*. New York: Routledge, 104–13.

Hacohen, A. 1999. Education in Israel and its expression in Israeli law. Ed. A. Peled. *The jubilee book of education for Isreal's 50th anniversary*. Israel: The Ministry of Defense, 85–107 (in Hebrew).

Halbwachs, M. 1980. *On collective memory*. New York: Harper & Row.

Hallak, J. 2000. Globalization and its impact on education. Eds. T. Mebrahtu, M. Crossley, and D. Johnson. *Globalisation, educational transformation and societies in transition*. Wallingford: Symposium Books, 21–40.

Halpin, D., and B. Troyna. 1995. The politics of education policy borrowing. *Comparative Education* 31(3): 303–10.

Hannay, L. M. 1996. The role of images in the secondary school change process. *Teachers and Teaching: Theory and Practice* 2(1): 105–21.

Hartley, D. 2002. Global influences on teacher education in Scotland. *Journal of Education for Teaching* 28(3): 251–55.

Helsby. G. 1999. *Changing teachers' work*. Buckingham: Open University Press.

Hlebowitsh, P. 1999. The burdens of the new curricularist. *Curriculum Inquiry* 29(3): 343–54.

Inbar, D. E. 1981. The paradox of feasible planning: The case of Israel. *Comparative Education Review* 25(1): 13–27.

——. 1996. The free educational prison: Metaphors and images. *Educational Research* 28(1): 77–92.

Israel Ministry of Education, Culture, and Sport. 1994. Bagrut [Matriculation] 2000: The report of the committee to examine matriculation examinations. Jerusalem: Shlomo Ben-Elihau (Editor).

——. 2001. Teacher education in Israel in changing times: A report of the committee for reform of teacher education. Jerusalem: Miriam Ben-Peretz (Editor).

Jackson, P. W. 1986. *The practice of teaching*. New York: Teachers College Press.

Jordan, S., and D. Yeomans. 2003. Meeting the global challenge? Comparing recent initiatives in school sciences and technology. *Comparative Education* 39(1): 65–81.

Kalmus, V. 2004. What do pupils and textbooks do with each other?: Methodological problems of research on socialization through educational media. *Journal of Curriculum Studies* 36(4): 469–85.

Kingdon, J. 1984. *Agendas, alternatives and public policies.* New York: Harper Collins.

Klein, Z., and Y. Eshel. 1980. *Integrating Jerusalem schools.* London: Academic Press.

Krueger, A. O. 2002. Supporting globalization. Remarks at the 2002 Eisenhower National Security Conference on national security for the 21st century: Anticipating challenges, seizing opportunities, building capabilities. International Monetary Fund, retrieved April 8, 2008: http://www.imf.org/external/np/speeches/2002/092602a.htm.

Labaree, D. F. 2000. On the nature of teaching and teacher education: Difficult practices that look easy. *Journal of Teacher Education* 51(3): 228–33.

Lampert, M., and D. Loewenberg-Ball. 1998. *Teaching, multimedia and mathematics: Investigations of real practice.* New York: Teacher College Press.

Leonard, L., and H. Salzman. 2007. The real global technology challenge. *Change: The Magazine of Higher Education* 39(4): 8–13.

Levin, B. 1998. An epidemic of education policy: (What) can we learn from each other? *Comparative Education* 34(2): 131–41.

Levin, B., and J. A. Riffel. 1997. *Schools and the changing world: Struggling towards the future.* London: Falmer.

Levin, T., and M. Ben-Peretz. 2007. Tensions between cultures in educating immigrants in Israel: From the melting pot ideology to a multiculturalism orientation. Paper presented at the History of Education Society Annual Conference: Education and Globalization, University of Birmingham, United Kingdom.

Lieberman, A., and L. Miller. 1984. *Teachers: Their world and their work.* Alexandria, VA: ASCD.

Light, D. 1980. *Becoming psychiatrists: The professional transformation of self.* New York: Norton.

Lindblom, C. 1990. *Inquiry and change: The troubled attempt to understand and shape society.* New Haven: Yale University Press.

Lo Bianco, J. 2004. *Processes of policy making and theories of public policy: Relating power, policy and professional knowledge in literacy agendas.* University of Melbourne, Center for Literacy, Montreal. Retrieved March 10, 2008: http://www.centrefor literacy.qc.ca/publications/lobianco.pdf.

Lortie, D. 1975. *Schoolteacher: A sociological study.* Chicago: University of Chicago Press.

Lucas, A. 1979. Environment and environmental education: Conceptual issues and curriculum interpretations. Kew, Victoria: Australian International Press.

MacDonald, J. B. 1975. Curriculum and human interests. Ed. W. Pinar. *Curriculum theorizing: The reconceptualists.* Berkeley: McCutchan.

Mazlish, B., and A. Iriye. (Eds.) 2005. *The global history reader.* New York: Routledge.

McCarthy, C., and G. Dimitriades. 2000. Globalizing pedagogies: Power, resentment, and the re-narration of difference. Eds. N. C. Burbules and C. A. Torres. *Globalization and education: Critical perspectives.* New York: Routledge, 187–204.

McClaren, M., and W. Hammond. 2001. The educational challenges of climate change: A framework for teaching about climate change. Eds. T. Grant and G. Littlejohn. *Teaching about climate change: Cool schools tackle global warming.* Canada: New Society.

McCloskey, H. J. 1983. *Ecological ethics and politics.* New Jersey: Rowman and Littlefield.

McIntyre, D. 2000. Has classroom teaching served its day? Eds. B. Moon, S. Brown, and M. Ben-Peretz. *Routledge international companion to education.* London: Routledge, 83–108.

Miller, J. P., and W. Seller. 1985. *Curriculum: Perspectives and practice.* New York: Longman.

Miller, S., and M. Fredericks. 2000. Social science research findings and educational policy dilemmas: Some additional distinctions 8(3). Loyola University, Chicago. Educational Policy Analysis Archives. Retrieved March 17, 2008: http://epaa. asued/epaa/v8n3.

Morrow, R. A., and C. A. Torres. 2000. The state, globalization, and educational policy. Eds. N. C. Burbules and C. A. Torres. *Globalization and education: Critical perspectives.* New York: Routledge, 27–56.

NAEP report. National Assessment of Educational Progress. 2003. Retrieved March 20, 2008: http://nces.ed.gov/pubsearch/getpubcats.asp?sid=031#.

National Association for Environmental Education. 1977. International Union for Nature and Natural Resources quoted in *Environmental education.* London, UK: Heinemann Educational Books.

Nias, J. 1989. Teaching and the self. Eds. M. Holly and C. McLoughlin. *Perspectives on teachers' professional development.* London: Falmer Press, 155–72.

Nicholson, C. 1989. Postmodernism, feminism, and education: The need for solidarity. *Educational Theory* 34(3): 197–209.

Niemi, H. 2000. Teacher education in Finland: Current trends and future scenarios. Teacher education policies in the European Union: Proceeding of the conference on teacher education policies in the European Union, and quality of lifelong learning, Loule, May 22 and 23, 2000. Portuguese Presidency of the Council of the European Union—Ministry of Education, Lisbon. The status and standard of Finnish science, 1997, study of a culture and society.

Nitzan Horowitz looks for tomorrow: Immigration [documentary film]. Channel 10, Israeli TV, Israel. (Broadcasted on June 30, 2008).

Northern Ireland Curriculum Council [NICC]. 1991. *Proposals for technology and design in the Northern Ireland curriculum: Report of the Ministerial Technology and Design Working Group.* Belfast: NICC.

Office of Economic Cooperation and Development. *Teachers Matter: Attracting, Developing and Retaining Effective Teachers.* Paris: OECD, 2005.

Organization for Economic Co-Operation and Development—OECD 1997. Parents as partners in schooling. Paris, France: The Center of Educational Research and Innovation.

Oulton, C., and W. Scott. 2000. Environmental education: A time for re-visioning. Eds. B. Moon, S. Brown, and M. Ben-Peretz. *Routledge international companion to education.* London: Routledge, 489–501.

Pedersen, S., and M. Liu. 2003. Teachers' beliefs about issues in the implementation of a student-centered learning environment. *Educational Technology Research and Development* 51(2): 57–76.

Phillips, D. C. 1995. The good, the bad, and the ugly: The many faces of constructivism. *Educational Researcher* 24(1): 5–12.

Putman, R. 1995. Bowling alone: America's declining social capital. *Journal of Democracy* 6: 65–78.

Raduntz, H. 2007. The marketization of education within the global capitalist economy. Eds. M. W. Apple, J. Kenway, and M. Singh. *Globalizing education: Policies, pedagogies, and politics*. New York: Peter Lang, 231–45.

Remennick, L. 2002. Transnational community in the making: Russian-Jewish immigrants of the 1990s in Israel. *Journal of Ethnic and Migration Studies* 28: 515–30.

Remillard, J. T. 1999. Curriculum materials in mathematics education reform: A framework for examining teachers' curriculum development. *Curriculum Inquiry* 29(3): 315–42.

Richardson, V. (Eds.) 2003. *Constructivist teacher education: Building a world of new understandings*. London: Routledge-Falmer Press.

Rosekrans, K. 2006. Using participatory research and informed dialogue to influence education policy: Lessons from El Salvador. *Journal of Education in International Development* 2(2). Retrieved March 17, 2008: http://www.equip123.net/jeid/articles/3/InfluencingEducationalPolicyLessonsfromElSalvador.

Sabar, N. 1990. School-based curriculum planning: Meaning of the concept, possibilities and dangers. Ed. I. Freidman. *Autonomy in education: Conceptual frameworks and implementation processes* (2nd edition). Jerusalem: Szoldz Institute, 130–44 (in Hebrew).

Sabar, N., and L. Dushnik. 1996. Principal lines in drawing a portrait of curriculum for 2020. Position paper presented for Israel 2020—Master Plan for Israel in the New Millennium (in Hebrew).

Sabar, N., J. Rudduck, and W. Reid. (Eds.) 1987. *Partnerships and autonomy in school-based curriculum development: Policies and practices in Israel and England*. Sheffield: University of Sheffield.

Sabar, N., and M. Silberstein. 1999. A uniform curriculum for multi-oriented learning structure. Ed. A. Peled. *The jubilee book of education for Israel's 50th anniversary*. Israel: The Ministry of Defence, 193–203 (in Hebrew).

Sarason, S. B. 1996. *Revisiting 'the culture of school and the problem of change.'* New York: Teachers College Press.

Schwab, J. J. 1964. Problems, topics and issues. Ed. S. Eilam. *Education and the structure of knowledge*. Chicago: Rand McNally, 4–47.

———. 1973. The practical 3: Translation into curriculum. *School Review* 81: 501–22.

———. 1983. The practical 4: Something for curriculum professors to do. *Curriculum Inquiry* 13(3): 239–65.

Shamai, S., and I. Paul-Binyamin. 2004. A model of intensity of multicultural relations: The case of teacher training colleges in Israel. *Race, Ethnicity and Education* 7(4): 421–36.

Shulman, L. S. 1987. Knowledge and teaching: Foundations of the new reform. *Harvard Educational Review* 57(1): 1–22.

Smith III, J. P. 1999. Tracking the mathematics of automobile production: Are schools failing to prepare students for work? *American Educational Research Journal* 36(4): 835–78.

Smyth, J., and G. Shacklock. 1998. *Re-making teaching: Ideology, policy and practice.* London: Routledge.

Sowell, E. J. 2000. *Curriculum: An integrative introduction* (2nd edition). Upper Saddle River, NJ: Merrill.

Spring, J. 2008. Research on globalization and education. *Review of Educational Research* 78(2): 330–63.

Steinhart, M. 2000. The perception of classroom situations by new immigrant pupils from different cultures. Unpublished doctoral dissertation, University of Haifa, Israel (in Hebrew).

Swanson, C. B., and J. Barlage. 2006. *Influence: A study of the factors shaping education policy.* Editorial Projects in Education Research Center (EPERC). Retrieved June 30, 2008: http://www.edweek.org/media/influence_execsum.pdf.

Tatar, M., and G. Horenczyk. 2003. Diversity-related burnout among teachers. *Teaching and Teacher Education* 19: 397–408.

Teacher education in Israel in changing times: A report of the committee for reform of teacher education. 2001. Israel: Ministry of Education (in Hebrew).

Townsend, T., and R. Bates. 2007. Teacher education in a new millennium: Pressures and possibilities. *Handbook of teacher education: Globalization, standards and professionalism in times of change.* Netherlands: Springer, 3–22.

Trends in international mathematics and science study (TIMSS). 2003. International Association for the Evaluation of Educational Achievement and National Center for Education Statistics. Retrieved March 17, 2008: http://timss.bc.edu/PDF/t03_download/T03_M_Chap1.pdf.

UNESCO-UNEP. 1978. *The Tbilisi declaration: Final report intergovernmental conference on environmental education.* Organized by UNESCO in cooperation with UNEP, Tbilisi, USSR, October 14–26, 1977, Paris, France: UNESCO ED/MD/49.

U.S. Law Dictionary. 2008. Retrieved May 14, 2008: http://www.uslaw.com/us_law_dictionary/i/Immigration.

Vanhuysse, P., and Sulitzeanu-Kenan, R. (in press). Teacher's PAT? Multiple-role principal-agent theory, education politics, and bureaucrat power. *Critical Studies in Education* **50 (2)**.

Vonk, J. H. C. 1984. *Teacher education and teacher practice.* Amsterdam, VU: Uitgeverij/Free University Press.

Vygotsky, L. S. 1978. Eds. M. Cole, V. John-Steiner, S. Scribner, and E. Souberman. *Mind in society: The development of higher psychological processes.* Cambridge, MA: Harvard University Press.

Wagenaar, W. A. 1986. My memory: A study of autobiographical memory over six years. *Cognitive Psychology* 18(2): 226–52.

Walker, D. F. 1971. A naturalistic model for curriculum development. *The School Review* 80(1): 51–65.

Wallace, R., and J. Kupperman. 1997. On-line search in the science classroom: Benefits and possibilities. Chicago: AERA (American Educational Research Association).

Watson, K. 2000. Globalisation, educational reform and language policy in transitional societies. Eds. T. Mebrahtu, M. Crossley, and D. Johnson. *Globalisation, educational transformation and societies in transition.* Wallingford, Oxford: Symposium Books, 41–67.

Weaver-Hightower, M. B. 2008. An ecology metaphor for educational policy analysis: A call to complexity. *Educational Researcher* 37(3): 153–67.

Webster's II new college dictionary. 1995. Boston and New York: Houghton Mifflin.

Wells, A., S. Carnochan, J. Slayton, R. Allen, and A. Vasudeva. 1998. Globalization and educational change. Eds. A. Hargreaves, M. Lieberman, M. Fullan, and D. Hopkins. *International handbook of educational change, part one.* Dordrecht: Kluwer Academic Publishers, 322–48.

WSIS. World Summit on the Information Society. 2003. Retrieved March 16, 2008: http://www.itu.int/wsis/index.html.

Yogev, A. 1989. From school reform to ethnic integration in Israeli schools: Social myths and educational policy. Eds. A. Yogev and S. Tomlinson. *International perspectives on education and society, vol. 1.* London: GAI Press.

Zerubavel, E. 1981. *Hidden rhythms: Schedules and calendars in social life.* Chicago: University of Chicago Press.

Zhou, M. 2003. Urban education: Challenges in educating culturally diverse children. *Teachers College Record* 105(2): 208–25.

Zimmerman, B. J. 2002. Becoming a self-regulated learner: An overview. *Theory and Practice* 41(2): 64–70.

Index

About the Author

Miriam Ben-Peretz is Professor Emeritus at the Faculty of Education at the University of Haifa. She served as Chair of the Department of Teacher Education and as Dean of the School of Education at the University of Haifa and also as President of Tel-Hai College. She was Head of the Center for Jewish Education in Israel and the Diaspora at the University of Haifa. Ben-Peretz was a visiting professor at several universities internationally. Her main research interests are curriculum, teacher thinking, teacher education, professional development, and policy-making. Among her numerous publications are *The Teacher-Curriculum Encounter: Freeing Teachers from the Tyranny of Texts* (SUNY, 1990), *The Nature of Time in Schools* (with Rainer Bromme) (Teachers College, 1990), *Learning from Experience: Memory and the Teacher's Account of Teaching* (SUNY, 1995), and *Behind Closed Doors: Teachers and the Role of the Teachers' Lounge* (with Shifra Schonmann) (SUNY, 2000). She has published widely in journals and contributed book chapters in Hebrew, English, German, and Spanish. In 1997, she was awarded the Lifetime Achievement Award by the American Educational Research Association (AERA) for her contribution to curriculum studies. She is the 2006 Laureate of the Israel Prize for Education Research.